SLOW COOKERS GO WILD!

Teresa Marrone

Creative Publishing
international

Minneapolis, Minnesota

Teresa Marrone is a freelance writer and editor, who has authored several cookbooks, including *Backyard Grilling, Cookin' Wild Game, Abundantly Wild, The Back-Country Kitchen,* and *The Seasonal Cabin Cookbook.* She lives in Minneapolis, MN.

Copyright © 2006 by Creative Publishing international, Inc.
400 First Avenue North, Suite 300
Minneapolis, Minnesota 55401
1-800-328-0590
www.creativepub.com

President/CEO: Ken Fund
Executive Editor, Outdoor Group: Barbara Harold
Creative Director: Brad Springer
Cover Design: Brian Donahue
Page Design and Layout: Pamela Griffith
Food Stylist: Rachel Sherwood
Production Manager: Linda Halls

Printed in China
10 9 8 7 6 5 4 3 2

SLOW COOKERS GO WILD!
by Teresa Marrone

All photographs copyright © 2006 Creative Publishing international, Inc.
Front cover photo: Pheasant and Dumplings: p. 91
Back cover photos: Pheasant and Noodle Soup: p. 17; Goose-Stuffed Peppers: p. 46.

Library of Congress Cataloging-in-Publication Data

Marrone, Teresa.
  Slow cookers go wild! / 100+ crockpot recipes for wild game / Teresa
Marrone.
     p. cm.
  ISBN 1-58923-239-9 (hard cover)
  1. Cookery (Game) 2. Electric cookery, Slow. I. Title.
  TX751.M3535 2006
  641.6'91–dc22   2005023737

CONTENTS

INTRODUCTION

Imagine coming inside after a cold day in the field—or a hard day at the office, for that matter—to a warm kitchen filled with the enticing smells of venison stew that's hot and ready to dish up. With a slow cooker, you can put your stew together in the morning—or even the night before—and it will be ready and waiting for you when you get home. And with this book, you can prepare that stew, or any of a hundred other tasty wild-game dishes, and have dinner on the table with almost no last-minute work.

This book is written especially for hunters and for those who want to prepare wild game in a slow cooker. Wild game is perfectly suited to the slow cooker, which excels at turning tough cuts of meat into tender morsels. If you have a slow cooker, chances are good that you have slow-cooker recipes for beef, chicken and pork … but how many do you have for venison, pheasant and wild boar?

Wild game has different cooking characteristics than domestic meat, and for best results, you need to take this into account when preparing it, whether in a slow cooker or on the stovetop. Beef, for example, has much more external fat and internal marbling than venison; the meat is basted and tenderized as it cooks. Venison is quite lean, with virtually no internal marbling; the external fat tends to be strongly flavored and is removed during butchering. It follows, then, that a recipe for nicely marbled beef steaks won't work properly if prepared with lean venison steaks.

Domestic poultry is generally sent to market at a very young age, when the meat is still quite tender; plus, due to modern agricultural practices, chickens and domestic turkeys get very little exercise, so have not developed any muscle firmness. Compare that to a wild pheasant or wild turkey, which spends its life running in the fields and flying freely. Wild birds have to work hard to survive, and their meat is much less tender than that of domestic birds; plus, wild birds are often much older when harvested than are domestic birds (and meat from older animals is less tender than that from younger animals, whether domestic or wild).

Of course, wild game also tastes quite different than domestic meat. Wild turkeys and wild rabbits, for example, have meat that is darker and much more flavorful than that of their domestic cousins. Many wild boars are descendants of domestic pigs, but the similarity ends there; boar meat is richer and nuttier than domestic pork, with a much more aggressive flavor that most hunters find irresistible. Birds like ruffed grouse and Hungarian partridge have no domestic counterpart; and who ever heard of raising squirrels for meat?! All of these wild foods are unique and delicious, and benefit from recipes that let their flavor to shine through. The slow cooker allows you to prepare wild game in a manner that retains all its natural flavor; most recipes are simple and quick to get started. What more could you ask for?

The evolution of the modern slow cooker

The first slow cooker was the original Crock-Pot® by Rival, which hit the scene in 1971. Even though other manufacturers quickly jumped on the bandwagon (or rather, into the pot), Rival so thoroughly dominated the market that Crock-Pot became synonymous with slow cookers (much as Kleenex® has come to be used as a generic word for tissues).

The first slow cookers were round, and held a modest amount of food; the crock was permanently attached to the base unit on most of these early models. Heating coils were generally on the bottom, so cooking was truly an all-day affair because the pots took a long time to get hot. Today's slow cookers range from grapefruit-sized to models large enough to hold huge roasts; round crocks are still available, but many models come in a convenient oval shape. Most slow cookers today feature a removable stoneware crock that is dishwasher-safe, which is a boon at cleanup time.

The most significant change between the slow cookers of yore and today's models, however, has to do with the heating system and, ultimately, the cooking temperature. Rather than heating just from the bottom, today's slow cookers feature heating elements that wrap around the inside of the base, cradling the crock and surrounding it with heat. Food heats more quickly, because there are more heating elements and they are interacting with a larger area of the crock. Modern slow cookers also cook at a higher temperature than older ("legacy") models; in part, this was a manufacturer response to concerns about food safety when it was determined that older, "cooler" slow cookers allowed foods to spend too much time in a temperature zone at which food-borne bacteria could multiply (the "danger zone" is 40°F to 140°F/4°C to 60°C; for safety, foods should spend less than 2 hours in this zone).

There is a simple test you can perform on an older slow cooker, to see if it meets modern food-safety standards. Fill your slow cooker two-thirds full of tepid (room-temperature) water, then cover it and turn it on the low setting. Heat for 2 hours without lifting the lid. After 2 hours, lift the lid and quickly check the temperature of the water with an instant-read thermometer. It should be at least 145°F (63°C). Next, re-cover the slow cooker and heat for an additional 6 hours (8 hours total). The water should be at least 185°F (85°C). Temperatures lower than this indicate that the slow cooker does not heat adequately, and should be replaced. (Most of this information comes from the Food Safety Project published by Iowa State University at www.extension.iastate.edu.)

In your own kitchen

Because of the differences between legacy and modern slow cookers, it's important to match the vintage of your slow cooker to the vintage of your recipes. If you use a modern, fast-heating slow cooker with a recipe that was written for a slower, cooler legacy model, your food will likely be overcooked and may even scorch or boil over. On the other hand, if you use a legacy slow cooker with a modern recipe, the food may not be fully cooked in the time stated in the recipe; in addition, it may not be heated quickly enough to ensure food safety. All recipes in this book were developed for, and tested in, modern slow cookers.

If you want to start dinner when you leave for work in the morning and have it ready when you return 9 hours later, you may find that modern slow cookers aren't slow enough! Foods may be done in as little as 6 hours (even on low), and this can be a problem if you're gone all day. Luckily, Rival has come up with a perfect solution: the Smart-Part™ Programmable Module. This gadget works with any brand of slow cooker. Plug the slow cooker into the Smart-Part and set the amount of cooking time; once the time is up, the unit switches the slow cooker to a "keep warm" setting, which can hold food safely for several hours without overcooking it.

Types of game to choose for the slow cooker

If you took a survey asking people what foods are best for preparing in the slow cooker, you'd consistently get two answers: beef stew and beef pot roast. That's because the moist, low-and-slow heat provided by the slow cooker is great for turning these less-tender cuts into melt-in-your-mouth delights. You might also hear that the slow cooker does a good job on cut-up chicken, standard beef and pork roasts, chops and casserole-type dishes.

Wild game is an even better candidate for slow cooking; as noted above, it is less tender than similar domestic meats, and benefits from slow, moist cooking. Because of the difference in tenderness, wild game requires longer cooking times than domestic meat, so you'll want to keep that in mind if you're trying to prepare wild game using a recipe that was written for domestic meat. It's best to start with recipes that were developed especially for wild game; then, when you're comfortable preparing a few of those, you can try your hand at adapting some of your favorite domestic-meat recipes.

I believe that more venison is prepared in the slow cooker than any other type of game ... and when I say venison, I am talking about not just deer meat, but that from any of the hooved big-game animals such as moose, elk or antelope (all of which are interchangeable in recipes that call for venison). Because a deer or other big-game animal yields so much meat, most hunters have an ample supply of it in the freezer. Plus, much of this meat falls into the less-than-tender category, making it perfect for slow cooking. (Save your prime venison roasts, such as the tenderloin and backstrap, for dry-heat roasting in the oven or a countertop roaster, or on the grill.)

Ground venison can be prepared with the same slow-cooker recipes used for ground beef; the only difference—aside from the taste—is that ground venison may not have any fat added to it, so it will require oil when browning in a skillet. Note that many food scientists now recommend that all ground meats be cooked prior to going into the slow cooker, because of concerns about bacterial growth during the relatively slow heating. This is of particular concern in a dish such as meat loaf, which uses a large amount of raw ground meat. You may want to avoid cooking raw ground meat in your slow cooker. If you do cook raw ground meat in your slow cooker, check it with an instant-read thermometer to be sure it reaches 165°F (74*C).

Squirrels and rabbits are a natural for the slow cooker, but you won't find many recipes that you can easily adapt for them because they take so much longer to cook than, say, chicken parts. Cut-up upland gamebirds and waterfowl work well in the slow cooker, and boneless, skinless gamebird meat works great in stews, casseroles and other simmered dishes. The slow cooker is not a good choice for preparing that whole prize turkey that you carefully plucked, nor for whole, skin-on pheasants or other gamebirds; the skin never browns and crisps as it does during oven-roasting, turning out wet and rubbery instead. Save those beautifully plucked skin-on birds for the roaster or oven.

SLOW COOKER SIZES AND CAPACITIES

Here's a list of currently available slow cookers, along with the name used in this book for each size. Metric conversions are based on information listed by the manufacturers; if metric information is not provided on the packaging, standard conversions have been used (rounded slightly).

	QUARTS	LITERS		QUARTS	LITERS
Mini	16 ounces	350 ml	Large	6	5.7
Personal	1.5	1.4		6.5	6.2
	2.5	2.4		7	6.6
Small	3	3	Medium roaster	6	5.7
	3.5	3.3		6.5	6.2
	4	4		8	7.5
Standard	4.5	4.25	Large roaster	16	15
	5	5		18	17
	5.5	5.2		20	19

About the recipes in this book

All recipes in this book were developed for, and tested in, modern slow cookers.

When a recipe calls for a gamebird, or small game such as a rabbit or squirrel, it is assumed that the game has been properly field-dressed and has been plucked, skinned or whatever is necessary to prepare it for the table. Skin should generally be removed from gamebirds and waterfowl; individual recipes will generally refer to this as well.

Feel free to substitute any type of hoofed big game for the venison that is called for in a recipe, as long as the cut is similar. For example, moose shoulder roast works just as well as deer shoulder roast in a pot roast, as long as the size is the same as what is called for in the recipe. Likewise, wild boar and javelina may be substituted for one another. Bear meat is rather in a class by itself, but if you have a freezer full of it, go ahead and try it in recipes that call for venison or wild boar; just make sure that bear, like wild boar and javelina, is always cooked to at least 165°F (74°C) due to concerns about trichinosis.

Most upland gamebirds can be freely substituted for another, as long as the size of the cut is similar; for example, you wouldn't want to substitute cut-up doves for cut-up pheasants, due to the size variation. But you could substitute Hungarian partridge pieces, or even Chukar partridge pieces, for pheasant pieces. If a recipe calls for boneless, skinless meat from a specific upland gamebird, you may substitute an equal quantity of boneless, skinless meat from any other upland gamebird. Ducks and geese are interchangeable in the same way; boneless meat from one does fine as a stand-in for boneless meat from the other, and as long as the birds are fairly similar in size, you can substitute parts—for example, a cut-up snow goose can be used in place of a cut-up mallard.

Some vegetable prep is assumed, and is not mentioned in the recipes. Onions and garlic are always peeled (unless specifically stated otherwise, as in Pheasant Braised with Whole Garlic on page 92); bell peppers are always stemmed and cored. Carrots and potatoes are generally peeled, but may be left unpeeled if you prefer; scrub them well before using. Turnips and other thick-skinned root vegetables are always peeled before further preparation. All fruits and vegetables should be well washed before cooking. By the way, a "rib" of celery is a single piece—not a whole bunch! When a recipe calls for vegetables to be diced, cut them into cubes or squares that are ¼ inch (6 mm), unless other measurements are given.

Let's get cooking!

No matter what type of game you've got in the freezer, you can prepare a delicious meal with it...just remember to take your time and go slow. I hope you enjoy the recipes in this book as much as I have enjoyed working on them.

> —*Teresa Marrone; Minneapolis, 2006*

CHAPTER ONE

Breakfast
and Brunch

Breakfast Casserole

Brunch Bread Pudding with Bacon, Fruit and Nuts

Hash Browns with Venison Sausage

Red Flannel Hash

Scrambled Eggs with Game and Cheese

Sausage, Potatoes and Sunny-Side-Up Eggs

Pinwheel Brunch Bread

BREAKFAST CASSEROLE

5 or 6 servings
Prep: 15 minutes
Cooking: 2 to 2 1/2 hours on high, or 4 to 4 1/2 hours on low
Slow cooker: Standard

Cooking on high gets this breakfast dish ready fairly quickly (for a slow cooker, that is!). If you're planning on brunch instead of breakfast, you can cook on low heat if you prefer. Juice and fresh fruit complete the meal; muffins or toast also go well.

1/2 to 3/4 pound (225 to 340 g) uncooked venison sausage (remove casings if links)
1/2 teaspoon (2.5 g/2.5 ml) butter or stick margarine
8 ounces (225 g) fresh mushrooms, sliced
2 green onions, sliced (white and green parts)
1 box (5 ounces/142 g) scalloped potato side dish
2 1/2 cups (590 ml) milk
6 eggs, or 1 1/2 cups (350 ml) liquid egg substitute
1/2 teaspoon (2.5 ml) dried herb blend
1/4 to 1/2 teaspoon (1.25 to 2.5 ml) Tabasco sauce, optional
3/4 cup (85 g/180 ml) shredded Cheddar or other cheese

In large skillet, cook sausage over medium heat until no longer pink, stirring frequently to break up. While sausage is cooking, rub inside of slow cooker with butter. Use slotted spoon to transfer cooked sausage to slow cooker; set aside. Pour off all but about 2 teaspoons (10 ml) drippings. Add mushrooms and green onions to skillet with drippings; sauté over medium heat for about 5 minutes. Meanwhile, in mixing bowl, combine sauce packet from boxed potato mix with milk, eggs, herbs and Tabasco; beat with fork until smooth.

Add cooked mushroom mixture to slow cooker with sausage. Add dried potato slices; stir to combine. Pour egg mixture evenly over all. Cover and cook until eggs are set, 2 to 2 1/2 hours on high or 4 to 4 1/2 hours on low. Just before serving, sprinkle with cheese and re-cover until cheese melts.

BRUNCH BREAD PUDDING WITH BACON, FRUIT AND NUTS

6 to 8 servings
Prep: 15 minutes
Cooking: 1¾ to 2 hours on high; requires stirring after the first 15 minutes
Slow cooker: Standard or Large

Surprise your guests with this brunch dish that is both savory and sweet, with just a hint of smoke from the bacon. For the fruit, I like a mix of craisins, golden raisins and diced apricots, but you can use a packaged fruit-bit mix or any diced dried fruit you like.

4 slices thick-cut bacon
½ pound (225 g) uncooked venison sausage (remove casings if links)
6 cups (215 g) dry cubed bread (see sidebar on page 123)
1 cup (235 ml/125 g) diced dried fruit (see note above)
½ cup (120 ml/50 g) coarsely chopped pecans or walnuts
2½ cups (590 ml) milk
4 eggs, or 1 small carton (8 ounces/236 ml) liquid egg substitute
⅔ cup (160 ml/135 g) sugar
½ teaspoon (2.5 ml) cinnamon
½ teaspoon (2.5 ml) rum extract or vanilla extract
2 tablespoons (30 g/30 ml) butter, melted

Spray inside of slow cooker with nonstick spray; set aside. In large skillet, fry bacon until crisp; drain, cool slightly and crumble. Add sausage to skillet with drippings; cook, stirring frequently, until no longer pink. Use slotted spoon to transfer sausage to slow cooker; discard drippings. Add bread cubes, fruit, nuts and bacon to slow cooker; stir to combine.

In mixing bowl, combine milk and eggs. Beat with fork until well blended. Add sugar, cinnamon and rum extract; stir well. Pour mixture over bread cubes. Cover and cook on high for 15 minutes. Stir well, then drizzle melted butter over bread cubes. Re-cover and cook on high for 1½ to 1¾ hours longer. Check during the last 15 minutes of cooking time to be sure bread isn't burning on the sides. You'll hear sizzling and will see deep browning along the sides of the cooker when you open it; the browned crust is delicious, but it can burn easily, so keep an eye on it. Remove cooker from base and let stand for 10 minutes before serving. Serve warm.

HASH BROWNS WITH VENISON SAUSAGE

4 to 6 servings
Prep: 15 minutes
Cooking: 2 hours on high; requires occasional stirring during last hour
Slow cooker: Small, Standard or Large

For quicker assembly in the morning, cook the sausage and vegetables the evening before. Serve this hash with scrambled or over-easy eggs and a pitcher of juice; I like salsa with the hash browns, but ketchup is also very good.

¾ to 1 pound (340 to 454 g) uncooked venison sausage (remove casings if links)
Half of a green or red bell pepper, diced
Half of a small onion, diced
1 package (1 pound 4 ounces/567 g) refrigerated hash browns, thawed if frozen
½ teaspoon (2.5 ml) dried oregano leaves
1 tablespoon (15 ml) vegetable oil
½ to ¾ cup (55 to 85 g/120 to 180 ml) shredded Cheddar cheese, optional

In large skillet, cook sausage over medium heat, stirring frequently to break up, until some of the fat is rendered. Add bell pepper and onion and continue to cook, stirring frequently, until meat is no longer pink and vegetables are tender-crisp, about 5 minutes. Drain and discard all but about 2 tablespoons (30 ml) of the drippings. Scrape sausage mixture into slow cooker, then use a large spoon to stir the sausage mixture so the sides of the slow cooker are coated with the drippings that remained with the sausage.

Add hash browns and oregano to sausage mixture; stir to mix. Use the spoon to push the mixture up the sides of the cooker, exposing as much as possible to the sides; this helps the potatoes cook and brown more quickly and evenly (see sidebar below). Cover and cook on high for 1 hour. After an hour, stir the mixture, and again push as much of the mixture as possible up the sides. Drizzle the oil around the sides of the cooker. Re-cover and cook for 30 minutes longer. Stir again, and push as much of the mixture as possible up the sides. Re-cover and cook for 25 minutes longer. Stir the mixture and pat it down evenly. Sprinkle with cheese. Re-cover and cook until cheese melts, about 5 minutes.

 CRUSTY POTATOES IN THE SLOW COOKER

Almost all modern slow cookers feature heating elements around the sides, rather than on the bottom. If you're cooking a potato dish like hash, you'll get crustier potatoes if you push them up around the sides of the slow cooker, where the heat is. For more even cooking, stir the food several times during the last hour of cooking; this exposes more of the potatoes to the hotter areas of the cooker. Use the high heat setting when you're cooking like this; the low setting doesn't get hot enough.

RED FLANNEL HASH

4 or 5 servings
Prep: 15 minutes
Cooking: 2 hours on high; requires occasional stirring during last hour
Slow cooker: Standard

Beets add color and character to this New England specialty; leftover cooked venison stands in for the traditional corned beef. Bake the potatoes the day before, and refrigerate until you're ready to assemble the dish in the morning. It's traditional to top each serving with a poached or fried egg.

4 slices bacon, diced
1 small onion, diced
1 clove garlic, optional, minced
¾ pound (340 g) leftover cooked
   venison roast, finely diced
1½ pounds (680 g) russet potatoes,
   baked, peeled and diced (about 3 large)
1 can (8¼ ounces/234 g)
   diced beets, drained*

1 tablespoon (15 ml)
   Worcestershire sauce
½ teaspoon (2.5 ml) salt
¼ teaspoon (1.25 ml) nutmeg
¼ teaspoon (1.25 ml)
   dried thyme leaves
¼ teaspoon (1.25 ml) pepper
2 tablespoons (30 ml)
   chopped fresh parsley

In medium skillet, cook bacon over medium heat, stirring occasionally, until bacon is beginning to crisp. Add onion and garlic and continue to cook, stirring frequently, until bacon is cooked and onion is tender-crisp. Drain and reserve all but about 2 tablespoons (30 ml) of the drippings. Scrape bacon mixture into slow cooker, then use a large spoon to stir the bacon mixture so the sides of the slow cooker are coated with the drippings that remained with the bacon.

Add venison, potatoes, beets, Worcestershire sauce, salt, nutmeg, thyme and pepper to bacon mixture; stir to mix. Use the spoon to push the mixture up the sides of the cooker, exposing as much as possible to the sides (see sidebar on page 11). Cover and cook on high for 1 hour. After an hour, stir the mixture, and again push as much of the mixture as possible up the sides. Drizzle about a tablespoon (15 ml) of the reserved bacon drippings around the sides of the cooker. Re-cover and cook for 30 minutes longer. Stir again, and push as much of the mixture as possible up the sides. Re-cover and cook for 30 minutes longer. Sprinkle with parsley before serving.

*If you can't find diced beets, buy sliced beets and cut into cubes.

SCRAMBLED EGGS WITH GAME AND CHEESE

4 servings
Prep: 15 minutes
Cooking: 45 minutes on high for preheating, plus about 1 hour on high for cooking; requires
  occasional stirring during 1-hour cooking period
Slow cooker: Personal (with removable crock)

Eggs scrambled in this way are more moist than skillet-scrambled eggs. This recipe won't exactly save you time compared to the standard scrambling method, but it requires little work and frees up the stove (and it works in a situation where no stove is available). The eggs can sit in the slow cooker on warm for up to an hour after cooking, making this a good dish to prepare in advance for brunch.

2 cups (475 ml) hot water
8 eggs, or 1 carton (16 ounces/473 ml)
  liquid egg substitute
3 tablespoons (45 ml) milk
1 tablespoon (15 ml) snipped
  fresh chives
1 tablespoon (15 ml) chopped
  fresh parsley

¼ teaspoon (1.25 ml) salt
A few grindings (or a pinch) of
  black pepper
¾ cup (180 ml/about 105 g)
  cooked, boneless diced game
½ cup (55 g/120 ml) shredded
  Swiss or other cheese

Add hot water to slow cooker. Cover and heat on high for 45 minutes; the water can heat for as long as 1½ hours if you like, until you're ready to cook.

When you're ready to begin cooking the eggs, remove the crock from the slow-cooker base and carefully pour out the water; pat the inside of the crock dry, taking care to avoid burning yourself. Spray the inside with nonstick spray; return the crock to the base. In mixing bowl, beat together eggs, milk, chives, parsley, salt and pepper until smooth; add game and stir gently to mix. Pour the mixture into the crock. Cover and cook on high for 15 minutes, then remove the cover, stir with a wooden spoon (scraping the sides and bottom to release any egg that has set), and re-cover. Cook for 15 minutes longer, then stir again. Repeat this at 10-minute intervals until the eggs are softly set; you will probably need two 10-minute cooking periods. When eggs are softly set but not firm, stir in the cheese; re-cover and cook for 5 minutes longer, or until eggs are desired doneness. Stir before serving.

USE A KITCHEN TIMER

A kitchen timer is one of the cook's best friends because it keeps you from forgetting to stir, turn or check foods for doneness (a timer has even become part of the kitchen gear I take when we're camping). It's particularly helpful in the Scrambled Eggs with Game and Cheese recipe, which requires short intervals of cooking followed by stirring. With the timer set, I can concentrate on other tasks until the timer's ring reminds me that I need to stir the food.

SAUSAGE, POTATOES AND SUNNY-SIDE-UP EGGS

4 servings
Prep: 15 minutes
Cooking: 2 1/4 to 2 3/4 hours on high; requires some attention during last 15 minutes
Slow cooker: Large oval

Use venison sausages that have been fully cooked during the smoking process for this dish. If you're using frozen potatoes, thaw them in the refrigerator overnight so you're ready to go in the morning.

2 teaspoons (10 ml) vegetable oil
4 smoked, fully cooked venison
   sausage links
1 package diced potatoes with onions
   (see note below), thawed if frozen

2 tablespoons (30 ml) water
1/2 teaspoon (2.5 ml) garlic salt
4 whole eggs
Salt, pepper and paprika

Pour oil into slow cooker, then use a pastry brush to thoroughly coat bottom and sides. Cut each sausage in half lengthwise, then cut each half into slices that are about 1/2 inch (1.25 cm) thick. Add sliced sausage, potatoes, water and garlic salt to slow cooker; stir well. Spray mixture generously with nonstick spray, then stir again. Cover and cook on high until potatoes are tender and browned in spots, 2 to 2 1/2 hours; stir once during cooking if possible (this helps ensure even cooking). When potatoes are tender, remove lid and stir potatoes. Working quickly, make 4 evenly spaced indentations in the potato mixture. Carefully break an egg into each indentation; sprinkle eggs with salt, pepper and paprika. Re-cover slow cooker and cook until whites are set but yolks are still runny, 7 to 10 minutes. Use a spatula to scoop out potatoes in 4 portions, each with an egg. Serve immediately.

Note: You'll find potato-onion mixes in the freezer case, as well as in the refrigerator case of most supermarkets. Package size varies from 1 1/4 to 2 pounds (567 to 907 g); sometimes, bell peppers are included in the mix. Any of these will work in this dish; you will probably need the longer cooking time for the larger package.

 OPENING THE SLOW COOKER TO CHECK PROGRESS

Generally, it's best not to remove the lid from a slow cooker during cooking; heat and moisture will escape, possibly increasing cooking time. This is particularly important when you're using the slow cooker like an oven, as in the Pinwheel Brunch Bread on page 15. With this recipe, look through the lid after the bread has cooked on high for 1 1/2 hours. If it looks golden brown and dry on top, remove the lid and very quickly poke the bread with your fingertip; if it's done, the top should spring back and the bread should not feel "doughy." If it's not quite done, re-cover the slow cooker as quickly as possible, and check again in 15 minutes.

If you're cooking soup, or a thick mixture such as chili or stew, opening the slow cooker has less effect on the temperature because the mass of the food will hold the heat better than the air that surrounds something like a loaf or a roast. Sometimes, in fact, it's a good idea to stir thick mixtures, to ensure even cooking and avoid burning caused by hot spots.

PINWHEEL BRUNCH BREAD

6 servings
Prep: 30 minutes prep the evening before final cooking
Cooking: 1 hour on low, followed by 1 1/2 to 1 3/4 hours on high
Slow cooker: Standard or Large, oval*

Preparation for this savory stuffed bread starts the evening before. The filled bread roll sits in the refrigerator overnight, then is baked in a two-phase process the next morning.

1 loaf (1 pound/454 g) frozen yeast bread dough, thawed
8 ounces (225 g) uncooked venison sausage (remove casings if links)
6 ounces (175 g) fresh mushrooms, coarsely chopped
1 red or green bell pepper (or a mix of colors), diced

All-purpose flour for rolling out dough
1 teaspoon (5 ml) dried herb blend
3/4 cup (85 g/180 ml) shredded mozzarella cheese
You'll also need: Standard-sized loaf pan

The day before cooking, begin preparing bread. Thaw and rise dough according to package directions; this usually takes 5 to 7 hours at room temperature. When dough has risen, punch it down and let it rest while you prepare the filling. Spray a standard-sized loaf pan with nonstick spray; set aside.

In large skillet, cook sausage over medium heat, stirring frequently, until it is broken up and beginning to lose pink color. Add mushrooms and bell pepper; cook until sausage is cooked through and vegetables are tender, 5 to 10 minutes, stirring frequently. Remove from heat; drain and discard excess grease and set sausage mixture aside to cool.

While sausage mixture is cooling, place bread dough on a lightly floured worksurface. Roll out to a rectangle that is approximately 11 x 15 inches (28 x 38 cm); position so one of the narrow edges is facing you. Sprinkle herbs evenly over bread. Spread cooled sausage mixture evenly over the bread, keeping 1 inch (2.5 cm) on each of the sides and 2 inches (5 cm) at the back edge clear of filling. Sprinkle cheese over filling, keeping edges clear as before. Roll bread up jelly-roll style, starting with the narrow edge facing you; as you roll, lift the rolled part slightly so you're not pushing all the filling toward the back edge. Pinch the seam and sides together very well, then place, seam-side down, in prepared loaf pan. Spray top of loaf with nonstick spray; cover with plastic wrap and refrigerate overnight.

When you're ready to cook, spray inside of slow cooker generously with nonstick spray. Work edges of loaf free, then turn loaf out onto your hand. Place, seam-side down, in prepared slow cooker. Prick the top of the loaf in 10 or 12 places with a sharp paring knife. Cover and cook on low for 1 hour, then increase heat to high and cook until top is golden brown and springs back when pressed with a fingertip (see sidebar on page 14); this should take 1 1/2 to 1 3/4 hours on high. Transfer loaf to a rack to cool for at least 15 minutes before slicing. Serve hot or warm.

*Don't try to prepare this in a legacy slow cooker that doesn't have heating elements up the sides; the bread will burn before it is cooked through if the heat is coming just from the bottom of the slow cooker.

CHAPTER TWO

SOUPS
and CHILI

PHEASANT AND NOODLE SOUP

6 servings
Prep: 15 minutes, plus 15 minutes shortly before serving
Cooking: 8 hours on low (can cook up to 9 hours), followed by 30 minutes on high
Slow cooker: Standard or Large

Feel free to substitute grouse, partridge or wild turkey for the pheasant; you should have about 2 pounds of bone-in pieces.

1 pheasant, skin and any fat removed, cut into serving pieces
2 carrots, sliced
2 ribs celery, sliced
Half of a small onion, diced
2 tablespoons (30 ml) minced fresh parsley
6 cups (1.4 liter) chicken broth
1 bay leaf
2 cups (475 ml) boiling water
2 cups (475 ml/90 g) uncooked curly egg noodles
½ teaspoon (2.5 ml) dried oregano leaves
½ teaspoon (2.5 ml) dried marjoram leaves
Salt and pepper

In slow cooker, combine pheasant, carrots, celery, onion, parsley, broth and bay leaf. Cover and cook for 8 hours on low; soup can cook up to 9 hours.

With a slotted spoon, transfer pheasant to cutting board and set aside to cool slightly; remove and discard bay leaf. Use slotted spoon to pick through soup mixture to remove any bones. Increase slow cooker to high. Add boiling water, noodles, oregano and marjoram; re-cover slow cooker. Remove pheasant meat from bones; discard bones and any tendons. Cut pheasant into bite-sized pieces and return to slow cooker. Continue cooking until noodles are tender; total cooking time on high will be about 30 minutes. Taste for seasoning, and add salt and pepper as necessary. Caution diners to watch for stray bones that may have escaped your notice.

Mexican Pheasant Chowder

6 servings
Prep: 15 minutes
Cooking: 5 hours on low, or 2½ hours on high (can cook up to 7 hours on low)
Slow cooker: Standard

This creamy soup is great topped with crushed tortilla chips or popcorn. A sprinkling of crumbled *queso fresco* (fresh Mexican cheese) is a nice touch also.

1 can (10¾ ounces/305 g) condensed cream of potato soup
1 quart (1 liter) chicken broth or pheasant stock (page 28)
¾ pound (340 g) boneless, skinless pheasant meat, cut into small bite-sized pieces
1 cup (235 ml/120 g) frozen whole-kernel corn, thawed
1 can (15 ounces/425 g) whole potatoes, drained and diced
1 jar (2 ounces/57 g) diced pimientos, drained
1 envelope (1.25 ounces/35 g) taco seasoning mix
1 cup (235 ml/227 g) sour cream (reduced-fat works fine)
1 cup (235 ml) nacho cheese dip*
3 tablespoons (45 ml) minced fresh cilantro, optional

In slow cooker, combine soup and broth, stirring to blend. Add remaining ingredients except sour cream, cheese dip and cilantro; stir again. Cover and cook on low for 5 hours, or on high for 2½ hours; the soup can cook for as long as 7 hours on low. Just before you're ready to serve, ladle about a cup (240 ml) of the hot soup into a mixing bowl; stir in sour cream, mixing well. Add sour cream mixture, cheese dip and cilantro to slow cooker; re-cover and let stand for 5 minutes before serving. If you have leftovers, reheat them gently but do not boil; the soup could curdle if overheated.

*Nacho cheese dip is a cheesy sauce that can be found with the snack chips at the supermarket. You could substitute half of an 8-ounce (225 g) package of pasteurized-process cheese (plain or with jalapeños), cut into cubes.

SCOTCH BROTH WITH WILD SHEEP

5 to 7 servings
Prep: 15 minutes
Cooking: 8 hours on low, or 4 hours on high (can cook up to 10 hours on low)
Slow cooker: Standard or Large

Wild sheep is particularly appropriate for this update on a traditional shepherd's dish, but you can substitute any other big-game meat, such as venison, antelope or bear, for the sheep. I like to grind fresh black pepper over my portion; fresh chopped parsley is also a nice garnish.

12 ounces (340 g) boneless wild sheep or other big game (see note above),
    well trimmed before weighing
1 quart (1 liter) beef broth
2 cups (475 ml) water
¾ cup (175 ml/145 g) pearled barley (not instant barley), rinsed
3 medium carrots, diced
2 small ribs celery, diced
1 medium turnip, diced
1 medium onion, diced
1 teaspoon (5 ml) salt
½ teaspoon (2.5 ml) dried thyme leaves
¼ teaspoon (1.25 ml) coarsely ground black pepper
1 bay leaf

Cut meat into small bite-sized pieces. Combine in slow cooker with remaining ingredients. Cover and cook on low for 8 hours, or on high for 4 hours; soup can cook on low as long as 10 hours. Remove bay leaf before serving. If soup is too thick, thin with a little hot water.

 REDUCING THE FAT

Unlike regular dairy products, condensed creamy soups can withstand long, slow cooking without curdling or separating; that's one reason they are used so frequently in slow-cooker recipes. Unfortunately, they are fairly high in fat. In recent years, Campbell's has come out with a line of reduced-fat condensed creamy soups, and these work just great in the slow cooker.

I also use evaporated nonfat milk in much of my cooking, to replace cream or half-and-half in recipes (don't try this for baking, though). A half cup (120 ml) of heavy cream has 5.5 grams; light cream has 2.9 grams of fat. The same amount of evaporated nonfat milk has 0.3 grams per half cup, and it works great in soups and casseroles.

Sour cream is available in light and nonfat varieties. I personally find the nonfat stuff to be chalky and prefer not to use it, but the light sour cream works fine in soups, casseroles and sauces.

THAI PHEASANT SOUP

5 or 6 servings
Prep: 15 minutes, plus 15 minutes shortly before serving
Cooking: 6 hours on low (or 3 hours on high), followed by 15 minutes on high
Slow cooker: Standard or Large

This recipe uses a few Thai staples that can be found in most large supermarkets, or at a specialty Asian grocer. Be sure to buy unsweetened coconut milk, not the thicker, sweetened coconut cream that is used for tropical drinks. The rice sticks used here are shaped like thin spaghetti with a rough texture; they are sometimes called *mai fun*. You can substitute any type of rice sticks you like; many kinds are available at Asian markets.

Boneless, skinless breast meat from 1 pheasant
2 small fresh hot red peppers, stems and seeds removed
1 strip lemon zest (yellow part only), about 1 x 2 inches (2.5 x 5 cm)
3 slices peeled fresh gingerroot, each about ¼ inch (6 mm) thick
1 clove garlic
1 quart (1 liter) chicken broth or pheasant broth (page 28), divided
1 can (7 ounces/199 g) sliced mushrooms, drained
2 tablespoons (30 ml) Thai fish sauce (*nam pla*)*
2 tablespoons (30 ml) packed brown sugar
2 to 3 ounces (60 to 90 g) thin rice sticks (see note above)
1 can (14 ounces/414 ml) reduced-fat unsweetened coconut milk (see note above)
6 green onions, sliced (white and green parts)
¼ cup (60 ml) whole fresh cilantro leaves (loosely packed, stems
   removed before measuring)
1 lime, cut into wedges

Cut pheasant breast into strips that are about ¼ x ¼ x 2 inches (6 mm x 6 mm x 5 cm); add to slow cooker. Slice hot peppers into very thin strips; add to slow cooker. In blender, combine lemon zest, gingerroot, garlic and about 1 cup (235 ml) of the broth; blend until smooth, then add to slow cooker. Add remaining broth, mushrooms, fish sauce and brown sugar to slow cooker. Cover and cook on low for 6 hours, or on high for 3 hours.

Near the end of cooking time, heat a saucepan of water to boiling. Break rice sticks into shorter lengths if you like (this makes them easier to eat). Add to boiling water, and cook until just done, 4 to 5 minutes; they will still be somewhat chewy. When noodles are soft, drain and add to slow cooker, along with coconut milk, green onions and cilantro leaves. Increase heat to high if necessary and cook for 15 minutes longer. Serve with lime wedges so each person can squeeze some into their soup.

*If fish sauce is unavailable, substitute light soy sauce; for a more authentic flavor, also add a pinch of mashed anchovy.

DUCK AND SAUSAGE GUMBO

8 servings
Prep: 45 minutes
Cooking: 8 hours on low, followed by 30 minutes on high
Slow cooker: Standard or Large

Gumbo is a traditional Southern dish that is somewhere between a soup and a stew. The roux—a mixture of flour and oil that is slowly cooked on the stovetop—is an essential part of the dish, as is the okra; both help thicken the gumbo and provide the traditional taste. If you don't have venison sausage, substitute any smoked sausage links.

½ cup (125 ml) vegetable oil
½ cup (70 g/120 ml) all-purpose flour
2 medium onions, diced
3 ribs celery, diced
2 green bell peppers, diced
3 cloves garlic, minced
Boneless, skinless meat from 2 wild ducks, cut into bite-sized pieces
1 pound (454 g) smoked, fully cooked venison sausage links, sliced
1 quart (1 liter) chicken broth
2 cans (14½ ounces/411 g each) diced tomatoes, undrained
1 tablespoon (15 ml) Worcestershire sauce
1 teaspoon (5 ml) pepper, preferably freshly ground
1 package (9 ounces/255 g) frozen sliced okra, thawed
½ teaspoon (2.5 ml) dried oregano leaves
Hot cooked rice

Prepare the roux: In a heavy-bottomed medium saucepan, heat oil over medium heat. With a whisk, blend in the flour. Cook, stirring constantly with whisk (or wooden spoon, once the roux has cooked a few minutes), until mixture is a deep golden brown and has a nutty smell; this will take 20 to 30 minutes. Add onion, celery, bell peppers and garlic; cook, stirring constantly, for about 5 minutes longer. Scrape mixture into slow cooker. Add remaining ingredients except okra, oregano and rice. Cover and cook on low for 8 hours. When gumbo has cooked for 8 hours, increase heat to high. Add okra and oregano. Re-cover and cook for 30 minutes longer. Serve gumbo in soup plates, atop a scoop of hot white rice. Many people enjoy Tabasco or other liquid hot sauce with gumbo.

VARIATION: GOOSE AND SAUSAGE GUMBO
Substitute 1 pound (454 g) boneless, skinless goose meat for the duck. Proceed as directed.

LENTIL AND UPLAND GAMEBIRD SOUP

6 to 8 servings
Prep: 15 minutes
Cooking: 6 to 8 hours on low, or 3 to 3¾ hours on high
Slow cooker: Standard or Large

Unlike most dry beans, lentils don't require pre-soaking prior to cooking. This is a good recipe to use with shot-up birds; be sure to pick out all shot and bone fragments before putting the meat into the slow cooker. If you prefer your lentils with a bit of firmness, use the shorter cooking time; the longer cooking time produces a texture like pea soup.

1 pound (454 g) boneless, skinless pheasant, turkey or other upland gamebird meat
¾ pound (about 2⅔ cups/340 g) dry lentils, rinsed and picked over
2 carrots, sliced ¼ inch (6 mm) thick
2 ribs celery, diced
1 small onion, diced
1 quart (1 liter) chicken broth
2 cups (475 ml) water
1 medium tomato, diced
2 tablespoons (30 ml) freshly squeezed lemon juice
½ teaspoon (2.5 ml) ground turmeric, optional (adds nice color)
½ teaspoon (2.5 ml) crumbled dried rosemary leaves
2 bay leaves
A pinch of sugar
Leaves from several sprigs fresh parsley, chopped

Cut pheasant into bite-sized pieces, being careful to remove any shot or bone. Add to slow cooker with remaining ingredients except parsley. Cover and cook on low for 6 hours, or on high for 3½ hours; the soup can cook on low for as long as 8 hours on low or 3¾ hours on high. Remove and discard bay leaves. Stir well; sprinkle with parsley and add salt if necessary just before serving. If soup is thicker than you like, simply add some additional hot water or stock to thin to desired consistency.

STEAK AND BARLEY SOUP

4 servings
Prep: 15 minutes
Cooking: 9½ hours on low, or 5 hours on high (can cook up to 11 hours on low)
Slow cooker: Small or Standard (double the recipe for Large slow cooker)

Venison from the shoulder, shanks or rump works well in this hearty soup. Be sure to remove any silverskin or tendons before weighing the meat.

1 pound (454 g) boneless venison roast or stew pieces
   (see note above, and sidebar below)
¼ cup (60 ml/35 g) all-purpose flour
Salt and pepper
2 tablespoons (30 ml) vegetable oil
1 quart (1 liter) beef broth
2 medium carrots, diced
1 rib celery, diced
1 small onion, diced
1 can (14½ ounces/411 g) diced tomatoes, undrained
¾ cup (175 ml/145 g) pearled barley (not instant barley), rinsed
1 tablespoon (15 ml) soy sauce

Pat venison dry; cut into strips that are about ¼ x ½ x 1½ inches (6 mm x 1.25 cm x 3.75 cm). In plastic food-storage bag, combine flour with salt and pepper to taste; close bag and shake to combine. Add venison; shake to coat. In large skillet, heat oil over medium heat until shimmering. Shake excess flour from venison and add to skillet; brown on both sides.

While venison is browning, combine remaining ingredients in slow cooker; stir to blend. Use tongs to transfer browned venison to slow cooker. Cover and cook on low for 9½ hours, or on high for 5 hours; soup can cook as long as 11 hours on low.

‮ GETTING THE MOST FROM VENISON ‮

If you butcher your own deer, you'll end up with lots of scraps. I like to keep two separate bowls for scraps as I go: one for scraps from less-tender areas such as the shoulder, and another for choice scraps from the backstrap or round. As soon as I've got a pound (454 g) or so of scraps in one of the bowls, I pack it into a labeled freezer-weight zipper bag and pop it into the freezer; later, I wrap the frozen package in freezer paper.

The less-tender scraps are great for turning into sausage or using in stews, while the choice scraps work well for dishes such as stroganoff, stir-fries and other dishes that don't get long, slow cooking. For the Steak and Barley Soup, choose stew scraps; the long, slow cooking will make them deliciously tender.

TACO SOUP

6 to 8 servings
Prep: 15 minutes
Cooking: 5½ hours on low, or 3 hours on high (can cook up to 7 hours on low)
Slow cooker: Standard or Large

This is a thick, hearty soup that is almost chili-like. If you like a bit of spice, use Mexican-style stewed tomatoes (with jalapeño) and both envelopes of taco seasoning mix.

1 pound (454 g) ground venison
1 teaspoon (5 ml) vegetable oi
1 can (14½ ounces/411g) stewed tomatoes, undrained
3 cups (690ml) beef or chicken broth
3 tablespoons (45 ml) cornmeal
1 medium yellow onion, diced
1 green bell pepper, diced
1 can (15 ounces/425g) pinto beans, drained and rinsed
1 can (15 ounces/425g) black beans with cumin, undrained
1 can (8 ounces/227g) tomato sauce
1 or 2 envelopes (1.25 ounces/35g each) taco seasoning mix
Garnishes: Diced avocado, shredded Monterey Jack cheese, sour cream, corn chips

In medium skillet, cook venison in oil over medium heat until no longer pink, stirring to break up. Drain and discard excess grease. Transfer venison to slow cooker. Add tomatoes with their juices to slow cooker; break up any large tomato pieces with a spatula or your hands. Add remaining ingredients except garnishes. Cover and cook on low for 5½ hours, or on high for 3 hours; the soup can cook up to 7 hours on low. Serve with garnishes.

TURKEY AND WILD RICE SOUP

6 to 8 servings
Prep: 15 minutes
Cooking: 8 hours on low, or 4 hours on high (can cook up to 9 hours on low),
  followed by 15 to 30 minutes on high
Slow cooker: Standard or Large

This delicious and hearty soup takes a quick bit of last-minute prep shortly before serving; other than that, it couldn't be any easier.

¾ **to 1 pound (340 to 454 g) boneless,**
  skinless turkey meat, cut into
  bite-sized pieces
½ **cup (120 ml/90 g) uncooked wild rice,**
  rinsed and drained
2 or 3 carrots, sliced
1 russet potato (peeled or unpeeled,
  as you prefer), diced
1 rib celery, sliced
Half of a small onion, chopped

1 can (10¾ ounces/305 g) condensed
  cream of mushroom soup
  (reduced-fat works fine)
1 quart (1 liter) chicken broth
1 can (12 ounces/354 ml) evaporated
  fat-free milk, or 1½ cups (350 ml)
  half-and-half
1 teaspoon (5 ml) dried herb blend
Salt and pepper

In slow cooker, combine all ingredients except milk, herbs, and salt and pepper. Cover and cook on low for 8 hours, or on high for 4 hours; the soup can cook for as long as 9 hours on low. When soup has cooked as directed, add milk, herbs, and salt and pepper to taste to soup. Re-cover slow cooker and increase heat to high (if necessary). Cook until mixture is hot but not boiling, 15 to 30 minutes.

ABOUT WILD RICE

True wild rice is a precious commodity that is quite different from the paddy-grown "wild" rice that is sold in most stores. Paddy rice is a hybrid of the original wild grain; it has been manipulated to make growing and harvest easier, and to produce a more uniform product. However, connoisseurs appreciate the flavor and integrity of true, hand-harvested wild rice, which is lighter in color and has a nuttier flavor than the commercial variety. True wild rice often has thicker grains, and may show a good deal of color variation within the batch. Paddy-grown rice is often artificially darkened by smoking, and the grains may be thinner and longer than genuine wild rice.

To obtain true wild rice, search out a Native American community in a wild-rice area (Minnesota and Wisconsin are prime areas), or look for a label that states that the rice is wild-grown and hand-harvested. I think you will be amazed at the flavor difference of the true wild variety; it's definitely worth seeking out. For mail order, try the White Earth Land Recovery Project, at www.nativeharvest.com. You may also be able to find a local wild-foods harvester who sells hand-harvested wild rice.

BEAR BORSCHT

6 to 8 servings
Prep: 30 minutes, plus 15 minutes shortly before serving
Cooking: 9 hours on low, or 4 1/2 hours on high (can cook up to 10 hours on low)
Slow cooker: Large

There are many ways to make borscht. Some variations use beets, while others use cabbage instead. This one features both, and substitutes rich, hearty bear meat in place of the beef short ribs that are usually used; you could substitute venison for the bear. Serve with thick slices of dark pumpernickel bread.

2 tablespoons (30 g/30 ml) butter
2 medium carrots, coarsely chopped
1 large onion, coarsely chopped
Half of a small head of green cabbage, cored and thinly sliced crosswise
2 cloves garlic, minced
1 1/2 pounds (675 g) boneless bear roast or steaks, well trimmed before weighing
2 medium beets (uncooked), peeled and cut into 1/4-inch (6 mm) dice
2 medium tomatoes, peeled, cored, seeded (see sidebar on page 29)
and cut into large chunks
1 large russet potato, peeled and cut into 3/8-inch (9 mm) dice
6 cups (1.4 liters) beef broth
3 tablespoons (45 ml) rice vinegar
1 tablespoon (15 ml) sugar
2 teaspoons (10 ml) salt
Sour cream for garnish

Melt butter over medium heat in Dutch oven or large pot. Add carrots and onion; cook for about 5 minutes, stirring occasionally. Add cabbage and garlic to Dutch oven; cook for about 10 minutes longer, stirring occasionally. While vegetables are cooking, cut bear meat into 3 or 4 large chunks and add to slow cooker. Add beets, tomatoes, potato, broth, vinegar, sugar and salt to slow cooker. When cabbage mixture has cooked as directed, scrape into slow cooker; stir everything well. Cover and cook on low for 9 hours, or on high for 4 1/2 hours; the borscht can cook as long as 10 hours on low. Shortly before serving, pull meat out of slow cooker and cool slightly; shred with 2 forks and return shreds to soup. Serve soup in wide soup plates, with a dollop of sour cream on each serving.

VARIATION:

If you're using smaller chunks of meat (such as stew chunks or trim scraps), dice the meat into 1/4-inch (6 mm) cubes before adding to slow cooker. Cooking time can be reduced to 8 hours on low, or 4 hours on high, when using diced meat. No additional shredding is necessary. This method is a bit more work up front (and I prefer the texture of the shredded meat to the diced meat), but it works just fine; choose your method based on the type of meat you have to work with.

VENISON STOCK (BROTH)

6 to 8 cups (1.4 to 2 liters) stock
Prep: 15 minutes, plus 45 minutes optional roasting time
Cooking: 12 to 24 hours on low
Slow cooker: Standard or Large

Choose bones that have some meat still attached; neckbones, backbones and ribs work particularly well. Browning the bones before adding them to the slow cooker produces a richer, more flavorful stock, but you can skip this step to save fuss. This stock is unsalted; add salt to taste when you're using the broth in recipes.

2½ to 3½ pounds (1.125 to 1.6 kg) uncooked venison bones (see note above),
   cut to fit slow cooker
1 large onion, quartered
4 carrots, each cut into several chunks
2 ribs celery (including leaves), each cut into several chunks
6 to 8 sprigs fresh parsley
8 whole black peppercorns
2 bay leaves
1 teaspoon vinegar, optional
6 to 8 cups (1.4 to 2 liters) cold water, or as needed

If you'll be browning the bones: Heat oven to 450°F (230°C). Place bones, cut to fit slow cooker, into a roasting pan. Roast, uncovered, until bones are nicely browned, about 45 minutes. Meanwhile, add remaining ingredients except water to slow cooker. When bones are browned, transfer to slow cooker. Pour a cup of the water into the roasting pan; stir to loosen browned bits. Pour mixture from roaster into slow cooker. Add enough water to cover bones and vegetables completely; the water should be an inch (2.5 cm), or a bit more, below the top of the slow cooker.

If you are not browning the bones: Combine all ingredients except water in slow cooker. Add enough water to cover bones and vegetables completely; the water should be an inch (2.5 cm), or a bit more, below the top of the slow cooker.

Cover slow cooker; cook on low for at least 12 hours, and up to 24 hours; you may need to add a little water if cooking for the longer time. The longer cooking produces richer stock. Unplug slow cooker at the end of cooking time. Use tongs to remove bones from slow cooker. If you want to pick the meat off the bones to use in casseroles or other dishes, set bones aside to cool; otherwise, discard the bones. Use a ladle to pour stock into cheesecloth-lined strainer that has been set over a large pot. Discard solids in strainer. Chill stock, then remove any fat from the surface.

Gamebird Stock (Broth)

6 to 8 cups (1.4 to 2 liters) stock
Prep: 15 minutes
Cooking: 8 to 24 hours on low
Slow cooker: Standard or Large

When you're boning gamebirds (pheasant, turkey, duck, etc.), save the back and other bones in a plastic bag; keep in the freezer until you're making a batch of stock, then combine them with wings and drumsticks, which are not as desirable for regular recipes as the more choice parts such as breasts and thighs. This stock is unsalted; add salt to taste when you're using the broth in recipes.

2 to 3 pounds (1 to 1.5 kg) uncooked gamebird pieces and bones
1 medium onion, quartered
4 carrots, each cut into several chunks
1 rib celery (including leaves), cut into several chunks
6 sprigs fresh parsley
6 whole black peppercorns
1 bay leaf
1 teaspoon (5 ml) dried herb blend
1 teaspoon (5 ml) vinegar, optional
6 to 8 cups (1.4 to 2 liters) cold water, or as needed

Combine all ingredients except water in slow cooker. Add enough water to cover bones and vegetables completely; the water should be an inch (2.5 cm), or a bit more, below the top of the slow cooker.

Cover slow cooker; cook on low for at least 8 hours, and up to 24 hours; you may need to add a little water if cooking for the longer time. The longer cooking produces richer stock. Unplug slow cooker at the end of cooking time. Use tongs to remove bones from slow cooker. If you want to pick the meat off the bones to use in casseroles or other dishes, set bones aside to cool; otherwise, discard the bones. Use a ladle to pour stock into cheesecloth-lined strainer that has been set over a large pot. Discard solids in strainer. Chill stock, then remove any fat from the surface.

CHILI-MAC

6 to 8 servings
Prep: 15 minutes
Cooking: 1 to 1¼ hours on high, or 2 to 2½ hours on low
Slow cooker: Standard

This dish is somewhere between a soup and a chili. It's simple food that's quick and easy to prepare;
kids will love it as much as adults.

1 pound (454 g) ground venison
1 teaspoon (5 ml) vegetable oil
1 rib celery, thinly sliced
1 small yellow onion, diced
1 green or red bell pepper, diced
1 jalapeño pepper, minced
1 quart (1 liter) beef broth
1 can (16 ounces/454 g) chili beans,
   undrained

1 can (14½ ounces/411 g) diced
   tomatoes with onion, undrained
1 to 2 tablespoons (15 to 30 ml)
   chili powder blend, or to taste
¾ cup (180 ml/90 g) uncooked macaroni
Garnishes: Shredded Cheddar cheese,
   oyster crackers, sour cream

In large skillet, cook venison in oil over medium heat until no longer pink, stirring frequently to break
up. Add celery, onion, bell pepper and jalapeño pepper; cook, stirring occasionally, until vegetables are
tender-crisp, about 5 minutes. Drain and discard excess grease. Transfer meat mixture to slow cooker.
Add remaining ingredients except garnishes; stir well. Cover and cook until macaroni is tender, 1 to 1¼
hours on high or 2 to 2½ hours on low. Serve in bowls with garnishes of your choice.

HOW TO PEEL TOMATOES

*Heat a pot of water to boiling. Carefully slip a whole tomato into the boiling water; boil for about 20 seconds, then
remove with a slotted spoon and hold under cold running water. Cut away the core with a paring knife; the skin
should now slip off easily. If I have a lot of tomatoes to skin, I generally do just one or two at a time; it goes quite
quickly, and I don't want to accidentally leave tomatoes in the boiling water too long while I'm peeling others.*

*For most recipes, you'll also want to remove the seeds: Cut the skinned tomato in half across the equator,
then turn the tomato cut-side down and gently squeeze to force out the pulpy seed mass (if the tomatoes are
not perfectly ripe, you will need to use your fingertips to pull it out). Discard the seeds, skin and core; cut up
the tomato as desired.*

STEAK 'N BEANS VENISON CHILI

8 servings
Prep: Overnight soaking, plus 30 minutes
Cooking: 9 to 10 hours on low
Slow cooker: Standard or Large

½ pound (225 g) dry pinto beans,
   picked over
1 large onion, diced
1 green or red bell pepper, diced
1 rib celery, diced
3 or 4 cloves garlic, minced
1 can (12 ounces/1355 ml) beer
3 to 4 tablespoons (45 to 60 ml)
   chili powder blend
2 tablespoons (30 ml) packed brown sugar
½ to 1½ teaspoons (2.5 to 7.5 ml)
   Tabasco sauce

1 teaspoon (5 ml) dried oregano leaves
1 teaspoon (5 ml) salt
1½ pounds (680 g) boneless venison
   steaks or roast, well trimmed
   before weighing
1 can (28 ounces/794 g) crushed
   tomatoes, undrained
½ cup (120 ml) hot water
Garnishes: Chopped onion, pickled
   jalapeño slices, shredded cheese, sour
   cream, crackers

Soak beans overnight, or use the quick-soak method (see sidebar on page 121). When beans are ready for cooking, drain and rinse in cold water. Transfer to slow cooker. Add onion, pepper, celery and garlic to slow cooker. In measuring cup, combine beer, chili powder, brown sugar, Tabasco, oregano and salt; mix well. Add to slow cooker and stir well. Cut meat into ⅜-inch (8 mm) cubes; add to slow cooker. Pour tomatoes over meat. Add water to tomato can and swish it around, then add that to cooker. Cover and cook on low for 9 to 10 hours, or until beans are tender. Stir well before serving with garnishes of your choice.

◥ ABOUT CHILE—AND CHILI—POWDERS ◤

"Chile" (with an E) refers to hot peppers, which may be whole or cut up, fresh or dried—even smoked. "Chili" (with an I) refers to a cooked, stew-like mixture that typically contains meat, peppers, onions, tomatoes, spices and sometimes—but not always—beans. "Chili powder" (referred to in this book as "chili powder blend") is a dried mixture of spices that generally includes ground chiles, cumin, salt, paprika and herbs.

There are many types of chile powders; the most common is ground cayenne, but there are a number of other delicious varieties. Ancho chile powder adds terrific taste, but little heat, to foods. Chipotle powder is made from dried, smoked jalapeños; unlike the ancho powder, chipotle powder packs plenty of heat. If you can't find these chile powders at your supermarket, try a Latin grocery, or order them from Penzeys Spices at www.penzeys.com.

By the way, paprika is another spice made of dried peppers. Spanish paprika is made from special red peppers that are smoked and dried over a hardwood fire; it is available in both sweet and hot varieties (try www.spanishtable.com for some excellent Spanish paprikas). Hungarian paprika is less smoky than Spanish paprika, and also is available in both hot and sweet varieties; Penzeys carries both. Either Spanish or Hungarian paprika have more flavor than the generic paprika sold at most supermarkets.

Texas Pride Chili (no beans)

5 or 6 servings
Prep: 30 minutes, plus 15 minutes shortly before serving
Cooking: 9 to 10 hours on low
Slow cooker: Standard

If you can get fresh poblano peppers, substitute two of them for the green bell pepper. This chili has no beans, but kidney beans are served alongside it as a garnish. The two chile powders give the chili a lovely, brick-red color.

2 large sweet onions, diced
3 tablespoons (45 ml) olive oil, approximate, divided
1 large green bell pepper, diced
4 cloves garlic, chopped
1½ pounds (680 g) boneless venison, cut into 1-inch (2.5 cm) cubes
1 to 2 tablespoons (15 to 30 ml) ancho chile powder (see sidebar at left)
1 teaspoon (5 ml) chipotle chile powder (see sidebar at left)
1 tablespoon (15 ml) ground cumin
¼ teaspoon (1.25 ml) cinnamon
1 bottle (12 ounces/355 ml) dark beer
1 cup (235 ml) beef broth
1 teaspoon (5 ml) salt
1 can (16 ounces/454 g) kidney beans, drained and rinsed
***Garnishes: Diced red onion, diced fresh tomatoes, pickled jalapeño slices, shredded
    Cheddar cheese, sour cream, chopped fresh cilantro***

In large skillet, sauté onions in 1 tablespoon (15 ml) of the oil over medium heat until just tender. Add bell pepper and garlic; sauté for about 5 minutes longer. Transfer mixture to slow cooker. Add another tablespoon (15 ml) of the oil to skillet, and increase heat to medium-high.

Pat venison cubes dry with paper towels. Add a loose single layer of venison to the skillet and cook until well browned on all sides, turning as needed. Transfer browned venison to slow cooker with slotted spoon; repeat with remaining venison and oil until all is nicely browned. When the last batch of venison is browned, sprinkle ancho and chipotle chile powders, cumin and cinnamon over venison in skillet; cook for a few minutes, stirring frequently. Transfer seasoned venison to slow cooker.

Pour beer into skillet, scraping to loosen any browned bits. Cook over medium-high heat for 5 minutes, then pour into slow cooker. Add broth and salt to slow cooker. Cover and cook on low for 9 to 10 hours, or until meat is very tender. When you're almost ready to serve chili, remove slow cooker liner from base, then use a wooden spoon to break up about a third of the meat cubes into shreds; this helps thicken the chili. Heat drained kidney beans in a saucepan with a little water (or microwave in a microwave-safe dish until hot). Serve beans with other garnishes, so each person can add what they choose to their chili.

CHAPTER THREE

SANDWICHES and SUCH

Sloppy Does

Wild Boar Burritos

Big-Game Tacos

Italian Garlic Hoagies

Venison Cheese Steak Sandwiches

Moose Au Jus (French Dip)

Blue-Plate Special: Open-Faced Turkey Sandwiches

SLOPPY DOES

6 to 8 servings
Prep: 15 minutes
Cooking: 5 hours on low, or 3 hours on high (can cook up to 7 hours on low)
Slow cooker: Standard

1½ pounds (680 g) ground venison
2 teaspoons (10 ml) vegetable oil
1 medium onion, chopped
Half of a green or red bell pepper, chopped
1 rib celery, chopped
2 cloves garlic, chopped
¾ cup (180 ml) ketchup
¼ cup (60 ml) beef broth

2 tablespoons (30 ml) packed brown sugar
2 tablespoons (30 ml) prepared mustard
2 tablespoons (30 ml) vinegar
1 tablespoon (15 ml) Worcestershire sauce
1 teaspoon (5 ml) seasoned salt
¼ teaspoon (1.25 ml) ground cayenne
    pepper, optional
Split hamburger buns

In large skillet, cook venison in oil over medium heat until no longer pink, stirring frequently to break up. Add onion, bell pepper, celery and garlic; cook, stirring occasionally, until vegetables are tender-crisp, about 5 minutes. Drain and discard excess grease. Transfer meat mixture to slow cooker. Add remaining ingredients except buns; stir well. Cover and cook on low for 5 hours, or on high for 3 hours; mixture can cook up to 7 hours on low. Spoon meat mixture into split buns.

WILD BOAR BURRITOS

4 to 6 servings
Prep: 15 minutes, plus 15 minutes shortly before serving
Cooking: 8 hours on low, plus 30 minutes on high
Slow cooker: Small or Standard

Look for the dried ancho chile in a Mexican market, or with the specialty produce at a large supermarket.

1½-pound (680 g) wild boar roast
2 dried hot red peppers, or ¼ teaspoon
    (1.25 ml) hot red pepper flakes
1 dried ancho chile, optional
Half of an onion, cut into 1-inch
    (2.5 cm) chunks

2 or 3 cloves garlic, sliced
¼ cup (60 ml) beer or chicken broth
6 to 10 flour tortillas
Garnishes: Shredded cheese, prepared salsa,
    chopped onions, chopped tomatoes

Cut boar into 1-inch (2.5 cm) chunks, discarding any tendons and excess fat. Place in slow cooker. Break peppers and chile into several pieces; add to slow cooker. Add onion, garlic and beer; stir well. Cover and cook on low for 8 hours, or until meat is very tender. Shred meat coarsely with two forks. Increase heat to high and cook for 30 minutes longer; meat should brown slightly. Heat tortillas briefly in microwave or oven. Serve meat with tortillas and garnishes.

BIG-GAME TACOS

8 to 10 servings
Prep: 15 minutes
Cooking: 4 hours on low, or 1½ hours on high (can cook up to 8 hours on low)
Slow cooker: Standard

Here's an easy taco filling that everyone will love. The refried beans give it a nice texture.

**1½ pounds (680 g) ground venison
or other big game**
2 teaspoons (10 ml) vegetable oil
1 large onion, finely chopped
**½ cup (120 ml) enchilada sauce
or taco sauce**
**2 tablespoons (30 ml) chili powder blend,
or to taste**

1 tablespoon (15 ml) ground cumin
1½ teaspoons (7.5 ml) salt
1 teaspoon (5 ml) paprika
1 can (16 ounces/454 g) refried beans
*For serving: Taco shells, shredded lettuce,
chopped tomatoes, diced onions,
shredded cheese, salsa*

In large skillet, cook venison in oil over medium heat until no longer pink, stirring frequently to break up; the texture should be fine. Add onion and cook, stirring occasionally, until onion is tender-crisp, about 5 minutes longer. Drain and discard excess grease. Transfer venison mixture to slow cooker. Add remaining ingredients except serving accompaniments; stir well to mix in beans. Cover and cook on low for 4 hours, or on high for 1½ hours; mixture can cook up to 8 hours on low. Stir before serving with taco shells and other accompaniments.

ITALIAN GARLIC HOAGIES

6 to 8 servings
Prep: 15 minutes, plus 15 minutes shortly before serving
Cooking: 8 to 9 hours on low, plus 30 minutes on high
Slow cooker: Standard

4-pound (1.8 kg) venison roast
5 cloves garlic
1 teaspoon (5 ml) dried marjoram leaves
1 teaspoon (5 ml) dried thyme leaves
**½ teaspoon (2.5 ml) hot red
pepper flakes**
2 teaspoons (10 ml) olive oil
2 cups (475 ml) beef broth
1 cup (235 ml) hot water

**1 envelope (1 to 1¼ ounces/32 to 40 g)
dry onion soup mix**
**1 package (16 ounces/454 g) frozen bell
pepper stir-fry mix, thawed**
*For serving: Crusty hoagy rolls, sliced
Provolone or mozzarella cheese,
sliced red onions, sliced tomatoes,
shredded lettuce, pickled hot peppers,
giardiniera*

continued on page 35

Pat venison roast dry with paper towels. In mini food processor, combine garlic, marjoram, thyme, pepper flakes and olive oil; process until very fine (alternately, you can press the garlic through a garlic press or chop finely by hand, then combine in a small bowl with herbs, hot pepper and oil). Rub garlic mixture all over roast. Add broth and hot water to slow cooker. Place roast in slow cooker; sprinkle with onion soup mix. Cover and cook on low until roast is tender, 8 to 9 hours. When roast is tender, remove from slow cooker; increase heat to high. Allow roast to cool slightly, then slice or shred and return to slow cooker. Add bell pepper strips and stir well; re-cover and cook for 30 minutes. Serve meat and peppers on split hoagy rolls, with desired accompaniments.

Venison Cheese Steak Sandwiches

6 servings
Prep: 15 minutes
Cooking: 6 1/2 hours on low
Slow cooker: Small or Standard

Creamy cole slaw, baked beans and corn on the cob are perfect accompaniments to these tasty sandwiches.

1 1/2 pounds (680 g) boneless venison steak, well trimmed before weighing
Garlic pepper, seasoned pepper or coarsely ground black pepper
Half of a can (10 3/4 ounces/305 g can size) condensed golden mushroom soup
1/3 cup (42 g/80 ml) shredded Parmesan cheese
3 tablespoons (45 ml) water
2 tablespoons (30 ml) Worcestershire sauce
1/4 teaspoon (1.25 ml) salt

1 small onion, cut into thin rings
1 green or red bell pepper (or a mix of colors), halved from top to bottom and sliced into half rings
6 hoagy rolls, split and toasted
6 slices (1 ounce/28 g each) Swiss or Muenster cheese
Garnishes: Shredded lettuce, sliced tomatoes, thinly sliced onions, sliced bread-and-butter pickles, mayonnaise, pickled hot peppers

Cut venison into 1/2-inch-wide (1.25 cm) strips. Sprinkle with garlic pepper; set aside. Spray inside of slow cooker with nonstick spray. Add half of the can of soup, and the cheese, water, Worcestershire sauce and salt to slow cooker; stir to blend. Scatter onion and bell pepper over soup; top with seasoned steak strips. Stir gently to mix. Cover and cook on low for 6 1/2 hours. Serve steak strips and sauce in rolls with cheese and any garnishes you like; for a nicer presentation, fill split rolls with venison mixture, top with cheese slices (cut in half to cover meat), and broil until cheese melts.

VARIATION: GOLDEN VENISON-MUSHROOM CASSEROLE
Follow recipe above, using full can of condensed soup. Increase water to 1/3 cup (80 ml). Eliminate hoagy rolls, cheese and garnishes. Cook mixture as directed; serve over hot cooked noodles or rice.

MOOSE AU JUS (FRENCH DIP)

6 to 8 servings
Prep: 15 minutes, plus 15 minutes shortly before serving
Cooking: 7 to 8 hours on low, or 3½ to 4 hours on high
Slow cooker: Standard or Large

A few pantry items form the base of a hearty dipping sauce. Choose a roast from the hindquarters, such as a rump or round portion, rather than a front-quarter roast. The hindquarter roasts have a finer texture and will slice more cleanly.

2- to 2½ pound (1 to 1.125 kg) moose,
   elk or venison roast (see note above)
Garlic salt, coarsely ground black pepper
   and dried herb blend
1 can (10½ ounces/298 g)
   condensed beef broth

½ cup (120 ml) red wine
½ cup (120 ml) water
2 tablespoons (30 ml) soy sauce
1 large onion, thinly sliced
Crusty French-bread-style
   rolls, or crusty baguettes

Remove any silverskin and fat from roast (see sidebar); pat dry with paper towels. Sprinkle generously with salt, pepper and herbs; rub seasoning into meat. In slow cooker, stir together broth, wine, water and soy sauce. Scatter sliced onions over the bottom of the slow cooker. Place roast on onions. Cover and cook until roast is tender, 7 to 8 hours on low or 3½ to 4 hours on high.

Fifteen minutes before serving, transfer roast to cutting board; let stand for about 10 minutes. Meanwhile, split rolls or baguettes most of the way through, leaving one side connected like a hinge; if using baguettes, cut into individual portions. Scoop out a bit of bread from the center of each roll, if you like (this creates a space for the meat). Slice roast thinly across the grain. Return sliced meat to slow cooker; stir gently to combine meat with juices. Fill rolls with meat slices and onions; serve juices from slow cooker in bowls for dipping.

REMOVING SILVERSKIN FROM VENISON

Silverskin is a thin but tough membrane that separates various muscle groups in big game. It looks like a shiny, silvery layer on the outside of the meat. It is tough, and can cause uneven cooking, so it should be removed before cooking.

A very sharp fish-fillet knife is the best tool to remove silverskin; the long, flexible blade allows you to remove the silverskin without cutting away too much meat. Removing silverskin is much like skinning a fish fillet; the knife should slip between the silverskin and the meat while your fingertips apply pressure to the silverskin, holding it in place.

Place the meat on a cutting board, with the silverskin facing down. Cut down into one end of the meat just to the silverskin, then grab the silverskin with your fingernails. Turn the knife blade sideways and scrape towards the other end of the meat, keeping the knife at a slight downward angle. Continue cutting the silverskin off in strips until the meat is clean. With a little practice, you'll be able to remove the silverskin in long strips with virtually no meat attached.

BLUE-PLATE SPECIAL: OPEN-FACED TURKEY SANDWICHES

5 or 6 servings
Prep: 15 minutes, plus 15 minutes shortly before serving
Cooking: 6½ to 8 hours on low, followed by 15 to 30 minutes on high
Slow cooker: Standard

Bone-in pieces add flavor to dishes like this, but the bones can fall out of the cooked meat into the gravy. If you use bone-in pieces, pick through the gravy very well with a slotted spoon and pull out any bones that have slipped out; also caution diners to watch for stray bones!

6 to 8 ounces (175 to 225 g) fresh mushrooms, sliced
2 tablespoons (30 g/30 ml) butter or stick margarine
2 pounds (900 g) boneless, skinless wild turkey pieces (breast halves and/or thighs), or
    2½ pounds (1.125 kg) bone-in, skinless pieces
Poultry seasoning or other seasoning blend
2 envelopes (generally about 1 ounce/28 g each, depending on brand) turkey gravy mix*
2½ cups (590 ml) water
2 tablespoons (30 ml) all-purpose flour, blended with ¼ cup (60 ml) cold water
For serving: Hot buttered toast, prepared mashed potatoes, cranberry sauce

In medium saucepan, sauté mushrooms in butter over medium heat until just tender; transfer to slow cooker. Season turkey to taste with seasoning of your choice. Place turkey pieces in slow cooker. Add dry gravy mixes and water to same saucepan, whisking to blend. Cook over medium heat, whisking constantly, until mixture boils. Pour gravy mixture over turkey pieces. Cover and cook on low until turkey is tender, 6½ to 8 hours.

When turkey is tender, increase slow cooker to high. With slotted spoon, transfer turkey pieces to cutting board and set aside to cool slightly. Use slotted spoon to pick through gravy in slow cooker to remove any bones, if necessary (see note above). Stir flour-water mixture into slow cooker; re-cover and cook until gravy thickens, 15 to 30 minutes. Meanwhile, remove turkey meat from bones if necessary; discard bones and any tendons. Using two forks, break meat into large shreds or chunks; return to slow cooker and stir gently. Prepare mashed potatoes and toast. For each serving, arrange toast on edges of plate. Scoop some turkey and gravy into the middle of the plate; place a generous spoonful of cranberry sauce alongside.

*If you like, use one envelope of turkey gravy mix and one envelope of mushroom gravy mix.

CHAPTER FOUR

MAIN DISHES

GROUND GAME

Meatballs and Marinara Sauce
Enchilada Casserole
Three-Bean Casserole with Venison
"Porcupine" Venison Patties
Swedish Meatballs
Spanish-Style Meatballs
Barbecued Meat Loaf
Venison Picadillo
Goose-Stuffed Peppers
Sweet and Sour Meatballs
Lasagna-Style Layered Casserole

BIG GAME

Italian Venison Stew
Venison-Mushroom Stroganoff
Pepper and Venison Goulash
French-Style Steaks with Wine and Brandy
Sweet and Tangy Asian-Style Venison
Southwestern Venison Stew
Sweet and Savory Round Steaks
Boar Chops 'n Kraut
Elk Swiss Steak
Stuffed Venison Rolls
Classic Venison Pot Roast
Herb and Garlic Game Roast for a Crowd
Savory Boar Roast with Apples
Simple Sauerbraten
Apple Cider Roast
Venison Roast Braised with Grenadine
Honey-Sweet Wild Boar Ribs
Barbecued Venison Ribs

SMALL GAME

Rabbit and Hominy Stew
Sweet and Sour Rabbit
Rabbit with Sweet Red Peppers
Creamy Mushroom Squirrel Bake
Classic Brunswick Stew
Country-Style Squirrel Stew
Squirrel or Rabbit with Mustard

GAMEBIRDS

Honey-Mustard Pheasant
Pheasant and Dumplings
Pheasant Braised with Whole Garlic
Stuffed Poached Upland Roll
Small Birds for Two
Dove and Cornbread Casserole
Curried Pheasant or Turkey
Birds and Biscuits
Pheasant-Stuffed Manicotti
Black Bean, Pumpkin and Gamebird Stew
Partridge with Apples and Bacon
Pheasant Legs Cacciatore
Duck or Goose Cassoulet
Shredded Duck Enchiladas
Orange-Sauced Duck
Duck or Goose and Dressing

MEATBALLS AND MARINARA SAUCE

6 servings
Prep: 15 minutes for sauce; 30 minutes for meatballs; 15 minutes during last hour of cooking
Cooking: 5 hours total on high; or 8 to 9 hours on low followed by 1 hour on high
Slow cooker: Standard or Large

Serve the meatballs and sauce with pasta, or use them to make delicious meatball sandwiches according to the variation below.

3 tablespoons (45 ml) olive oil, divided
4 cloves garlic, coarsely chopped
1 can (28 ounces/793 g) whole
   plum tomatoes, undrained
1 can (28 ounces/793 g) crushed
   plum tomatoes, undrained
1 teaspoon (5 ml) salt
¼ teaspoon (1.25 ml) hot red pepper flakes
¼ cup (60 ml) chopped fresh basil
1 teaspoon (5 ml) dried oregano leaves
Hot cooked spaghetti or pasta of your choice

MEATBALLS:
1 egg
¼ cup (60 ml) Italian-seasoned
   bread crumbs
1 pound (454 g) ground venison
½ pound (225 g) ground pork
¼ cup (30 g/60 ml) finely grated
Parmesan cheese
1 clove garlic, minced
¼ teaspoon (1.25 ml) salt

In small skillet, heat 2 tablespoons (30 ml) of the oil over medium heat until warm. Add garlic; sauté until garlic just begins to turn golden. Drain juice from whole tomatoes; add juice to skillet. Cook, stirring frequently, until liquid cooks away and sauce thickens, about 5 minutes. Scrape mixture into slow cooker. Add whole tomatoes to slow cooker, breaking them up slightly with your hands. Add crushed tomatoes, salt and pepper flakes to slow cooker. Cover and cook the sauce on high for 4 hours, or on low for 8 hours (sauce can cook up to 9 hours on low); stir once during cooking if possible.

The meatballs can be mixed and shaped right after you start the sauce, and then refrigerated until later; or, you can mix the meatballs after the sauce has cooked. (It's important that the meatballs be hot from the skillet when they are added to the sauce; if you cook the meatballs in advance and refrigerate them, the sauce will cool down too much.) To prepare the meatballs: In mixing bowl, beat egg with fork. Stir in bread crumbs; let stand for 5 minutes. Add remaining meatball ingredients, mixing well with your hands. Shape into firmly packed balls that are 1½ inches (4 cm) in diameter. If preparing in advance, place uncooked meatballs in dish; cover and refrigerate until needed.

When the sauce has cooked as directed, heat remaining 1 tablespoon (15 ml) of the oil in large skillet over medium-high heat. Add meatballs in a single layer and brown very well on all sides. Transfer meatballs to slow cooker with sauce; add basil and oregano and stir gently. Increase heat to high if necessary, and cook for 1 hour longer. Serve over hot cooked spaghetti.

VARIATION: MEATBALL SANDWICHES

Increase ground venison to 1¼ pounds (570 g). Prepare sauce and meatballs as directed above; omit pasta. Spoon sauce and meatballs into split French rolls or hoagie rolls, spooning in plenty of sauce. Top each open sandwich with a slice of mozzarella or Provolone cheese (broil open-faced sandwiches until cheese melts, if you like). Serve with pickled peppers or other condiments of your choice; pour remaining sauce in a bowl for dipping.

ENCHILADA CASSEROLE

5 or 6 servings
Prep: 30 minutes
Cooking: 5 hours on low (can cook up to 6 hours)
Slow cooker: Standard

Here's a hearty and satisfying casserole for deer camp. For a more complete meal, serve it with yellow Mexican rice and a tossed salad; some sliced avocados would be a nice addition to the salad.

1 pound (454 g) ground venison
1 teaspoon (5 ml) vegetable oil
1 small onion, diced
Half of a green bell pepper, diced
1 can (15½ ounces/439 g)
   pinto beans, drained and rinsed
1 can (15 ounces/425 g) black beans,
   drained and rinsed

1 can (14½ ounces/411 g) diced tomatoes
   with green chile, undrained
1¼ cups (300 ml) enchilada sauce
6 corn tortillas (6-inch/15-cm diameter)
2 cups (8 ounces/230 g/475 ml)
   shredded Colby-Jack cheese blend
Optional garnish: 2 green onions,
   sliced (white and green parts)

In large skillet, cook venison in oil over medium heat until no longer pink, stirring frequently to break up. Add onion and bell pepper; cook, stirring occasionally, until vegetables are tender-crisp, about 5 minutes. Drain and discard excess grease. Add pinto and black beans, undrained tomatoes and enchilada sauce to skillet; stir well. Reduce heat to medium and cook for about 10 minutes, stirring once or twice. Meanwhile, cut 2 of the tortillas in half; set aside.

Spray inside of slow cooker with nonstick spray. Add one-quarter of the venison mixture to slow cooker. Top with a whole and a half tortilla; sprinkle one-quarter of the cheese over tortillas. Repeat layers until all ingredients are used except the last 1½ tortillas and one-quarter of the cheese. Cut remaining 1½ tortillas into 1-inch (2.5-cm) squares; scatter over top layer of venison mixture. Top with remaining cheese. Cover and cook on low for 5 hours; the casserole can cook up to 6 hours on low. Sprinkle with green onions before serving.

THREE-BEAN CASSEROLE WITH VENISON

8 servings
Prep: 15 minutes
Cooking: 6 hours on low, or 3 hours on high (can cook up to 8 hours on low)
Slow cooker: Standard or Large

These tangy, sweet beans, spiked with venison and bacon, will be one of the first things to go at a potluck dinner. Use any type of ground big game that you have on hand—elk, moose, bear, antelope etc.

continued on page 41

6 slices bacon, chopped
1 to 1½ pounds (454 to 680 g)
  ground venison
1 medium onion, diced
1 can (16 ounces/454 g)
  baked beans, undrained
1 can (16 ounces/454 g) kidney beans,
  drained and rinsed

1 can (15½ ounces/439 g) butter beans,
  drained and rinsed
1 can (8 ounces/227 g) tomato sauce
⅓ cup (80 ml/73 g) packed brown sugar
2 tablespoons (30 ml) juice
  from a jar of pickles
1 tablespoon (15 ml) Worcestershire sauce
½ teaspoon (2.5 ml) prepared mustard

In large skillet, cook bacon over medium heat, stirring frequently, until crisp. Use slotted spoon to transfer bacon to slow cooker. Drain all but 1 teaspoon (5 ml) drippings from skillet. Add venison and onions to skillet. Cook over medium heat until venison is no longer pink, stirring frequently to break up. Use slotted spoon to transfer venison mixture to slow cooker; discard any remaining drippings. Add remaining ingredients to slow cooker; stir well. Cover and cook for 6 hours on low, or 3 hours on high; the casserole can cook up to 8 hours on low.

"Porcupine" Venison Patties

4 servings
Prep: 15 minutes
Cooking: 2½ to 2¾ hours on high
Slow cooker: Standard or Large

No, there's no porcupine meat in this recipe … just venison! This is based on a meatball dish my mom used to make when I was a kid. We loved these "prickly-looking" meatballs, which were covered in raw rice before cooking. Here's an adapted version for patties, done in the slow cooker. (Please read about preparing raw ground meat in the slow cooker, page 6.)

1 small onion, diced
1 pound (454 g) ground venison
1 teaspoon (5 ml) Worcestershire sauce
½ teaspoon (2.5 ml) seasoned salt
½ teaspoon (2.5 ml) dry mustard powder

⅓ cup (80 ml) long-grain rice (uncooked)
⅓ cup (80 ml) barbecue sauce
2 teaspoons (10 ml) all-purpose flour
1 can (14½ ounces/411g)
  stewed tomatoes, undrained

Spray inside of slow cooker with nonstick spray. Scatter onions evenly in slow cooker; set aside. In mixing bowl, mix together venison, Worcestershire sauce, salt and mustard with your hands. Shape into 4 patties, each about 4 x 3 x ¾ inches (10 x 7.5 x 2 cm). Place rice in flat dish; press patties into rice, coating both sides. Arrange coated patties in slow cooker over onions, reshaping patties slightly as needed to fit in a single layer. In mixing bowl used to mix the meat, combine barbecue sauce and flour; stir until blended. Add tomatoes and their juices, stirring to mix. Pour tomato mixture evenly over patties. Cover slow cooker; cook on high for 2½ to 2¾ hours, or until rice is tender and patties are cooked through.

SWEDISH MEATBALLS

4 to 6 main-dish servings, or 8 to 10 appetizer servings
Prep: 30 minutes
Cooking: 4 hours on low, or 2 hours on high
Slow cooker: Standard or Large

Serve these meatballs as a main course with mashed potatoes, or on a buffet table as an appetizer. Cranberry relish, pickled beets and dill pickles go very well with the meatballs.

½ **cup (120 ml) breadcrumbs**
½ **cup (120 ml) half-and-half**
½ **teaspoon (2.5 ml) salt**
¼ **teaspoon (1.25 ml) white pepper**
⅛ **teaspoon (.625 ml) nutmeg**
1 small red onion, minced
2 teaspoons (10 g/10 ml) butter
1 egg
1 pound (454 g) ground venison
½ **pound (225 g) ground pork**

1 tablespoon (15 ml) honey
1 tablespoon (15 ml) vegetable oil
1 cup (235 ml) chicken broth
1 can (5 ounces/147 ml) evaporated milk
¼ **cup (60 ml) currant jelly or smooth cranberry sauce**
2 tablespoons (30 ml) all-purpose flour
1 tablespoon (15 ml) juice from a jar of pickles

In large mixing bowl, stir together breadcrumbs, half-and-half, salt, pepper and nutmeg; set aside. In large skillet, sauté onion in butter over medium heat until tender; remove from heat and allow to cool slightly.

Add egg to breadcrumbs and beat with a fork until blended. Add venison, pork, honey and cooled onion to breadcrumb mixture; mix very well with your hands. Shape into 1-inch (2.5-cm) meatballs (mixture will be very soft; see sidebar for tips on making meatballs). Heat oil in same skillet over medium heat. Add half of the meatballs; cook over medium-low heat until lightly browned on all sides, turning as needed. Use slotted spoon to transfer cooked meatballs to slow cooker; repeat with remaining meatballs. When all meatballs have been transferred to slow cooker, add broth, milk, jelly, flour and pickle juice to skillet, whisking to blend flour. Cook over medium heat for about 5 minutes, stirring frequently. Pour sauce over meatballs in slow cooker. Cover and cook on low for 4 hours, or on high for 2 hours.

MEATBALL TIPS

• *Meatballs are easiest to shape with clean, wet hands, particularly when you're working with a soft meatball mixture such as the Swedish Meatballs. If your hands become sticky after rolling a few meatballs, rinse them and continue with clean, wet hands.*

• *Place meatballs in the warm skillet as you roll them, distributing them loosely in the skillet rather than packing them in tightly (if you pack them in too tightly, you won't have room to turn them). As you place each meatball in the skillet, work from one "zone" of the skillet to the opposite edge. By the time you add the meatballs to the last zone, the meatballs that went into the skillet first will probably be ready to turn.*

• *When a meatball is properly browned, it will release naturally from the skillet and can be rolled over (rather than picked up and flipped). This is a more gentle method of turning, and works best with delicate meatballs such as the Swedish Meatballs. If the meatball doesn't release with a gentle prod, it isn't ready to turn.*

SPANISH-STYLE MEATBALLS

3 or 4 main-dish servings, or 6 appetizer servings
Prep: 30 minutes
Cooking: 4 hours on low, or 2 hours on high (can cook up to 5 hours on low)
Slow cooker: Standard

This can be served as a main course with rice or potatoes; it also makes a nice addition to a mixed selection of tapas (Spanish appetizers). It's best to prepare this in a standard-sized slow cooker, not a large one. If you have a large slow cooker, double the recipe to prevent overcooking caused by a too-thin layer of meatballs and sauce.

MEATBALLS:
1 egg
1/3 cup (80 ml) bread crumbs
1 pound (454 g) ground venison
1/4 pound (115 g) ground pork
1/2 teaspoon (2.5 ml) salt
All-purpose flour for dredging

SAUCE:
1 tablespoon plus 1 teaspoon (20 ml) olive oil, divided
1/3 cup (80 ml) diced onion
1 1/2 cups (350 ml) chicken broth
1/3 cup (80 ml) dry white wine
3 medium tomatoes, peeled,* seeded and diced

1/2 cup (120 ml) frozen green peas, thawed (do not substitute canned peas)
3 tablespoons (45 ml) finely chopped blanched almonds
1 teaspoon (5 ml) paprika, preferably sweet Spanish
1 teaspoon (5 ml) cocoa powder (the kind used for baking)
1/2 teaspoon (2.5 ml) salt
A pinch of saffron (crumble if using saffron threads)
2 cloves garlic, minced or pressed
1 bay leaf
1 dried hot red pepper, optional
Chopped fresh parsley for garnish

To prepare meatballs: In mixing bowl, beat egg with fork. Stir in bread crumbs; let stand for 5 minutes. Add venison, pork and salt; mix well with your hands. Shape into firmly packed balls that are 1 1/2 inches (4 cm) in diameter. Roll in flour, shaking off excess. Heat 1 tablespoon of the oil in large skillet over medium-high heat; add meatballs and brown on all sides. Transfer meatballs to slow cooker.

Add remaining 1 teaspoon (5 ml) of the oil to skillet. Add onion; sauté over medium heat until just tender. Add broth, wine and tomatoes to skillet and cook for 5 minutes, stirring to loosen browned bits. Add remaining ingredients except parsley to skillet; stir gently to mix. Pour tomato mixture over meatballs. Cover and cook on low for 4 hours, or on high for 2 hours; the meatballs can cook up to 5 hours on low. Remove and discard bay leaf and hot pepper; sprinkle with parsley before serving.

*See sidebar on page 29 for instructions on how to peel tomatoes.

BARBECUED MEAT LOAF

6 servings
Prep: 15 minutes
Cooking: 2 1/2 to 3 1/4 hours on low
Slow cooker: Standard or Large

Please see page 6 about preparing ground meat in the slow cooker. For myself, I feel that proper field-dressing techniques and butchering greatly reduce the chance of bacterial contamination, and I am not concerned about preparing venison meat loaf in my modern slow cooker.

1 egg
1/2 cup (120 ml) barbecue sauce, divided
1/2 cup (120 ml) seasoned breadcrumbs
1 small onion, chopped
1 rib celery, finely chopped

1/2 teaspoon (2.5 ml) garlic salt
1/4 teaspoon (1.25 ml) pepper
2 pounds (900 g) ground venison*
Foil strips for lifting (see below)

In mixing bowl, beat egg with fork. Stir in half of the barbecue sauce. Add breadcrumbs, onion, celery, garlic salt and pepper; mix well. Set aside for 5 minutes. Crumble ground venison into mixture; mix gently but thoroughly with your hands.

Prepare foil strips as described in sidebar; arrange strips on worksurface. Shape meat into oval or round loaf that will fit into your cooker with space all around; pack meat firmly. Use foil strips to lift loaf into cooker. Spread remaining barbecue sauce evenly over top of loaf. Cover and cook on low until center of meatloaf reads 165°F (74°C) on an instant-read thermometer; total cooking time will be 2 1/2 to 3 1/4 hours, and the meatloaf can stay in the cooker up to 45 minutes after it is done. Use foil strips to transfer meat loaf to serving platter; let rest 10 minutes before slicing.

*If your ground venison is very low in fat, substitute 1 pound (454 g) of regular ground beef (85% lean) for 1 pound (454 g) of the venison.

USING FOIL STRIPS TO LIFT FOODS

Foods such as meat loaf can be difficult to lift from a slow cooker, because you can't get a spatula down inside the crock and underneath the finished food. To solve this problem, arrange long strips of foil under the food before adding it to the slow cooker; when the food is cooked, grasp all the strips together to lift it out.

If your cooker is oval, use 2 strips; for a round cooker, 3 strips work better. Tear off strips of 12-inch-wide (30 cm) foil that are long enough to lie flat in the bottom of the slow cooker and run up both sides, with additional foil left on each end (this excess creates "handles" that you'll use for lifting).

Fold each length of foil in half vertically, then in half again, to form 3-inch-wide (8 cm) strips. For an oval cooker, place the 2 strips on your worksurface, parallel to one another; for a round cooker, place them on your worksurface in a starburst pattern. Place the meatloaf, or other food to be cooked, onto the strips. Wrap strips up along the sides, then use the long ends to lift the food up and into the slow cooker. Roll the excess foil down along the inside edges of the slow cooker so they don't interfere with the lid. When the food is cooked, open the lid and allow the steam to dissipate; then, use tongs to unroll the foil (the tongs protect your fingers from heat). Grasp the ends of all the foil strips, and carefully lift the food out of the slow cooker; Gently pull out the foil strips before cutting the food.

VENISON PICADILLO

4 servings
Prep: 15 minutes
Cooking: 4 hours on low, or 2 hours on high (can cook up to 6 hours on low)
Slow cooker: Small or Standard

In Cuba, this dish is made with flavorful ground beef chuck. Venison contributes even more flavor, and stands up well to the assertive flavors of this traditional dish. Serve Picadillo with black beans and rice; for a truly authentic feast, fry up some slices of ripe plantain. Picadillo also makes an outstanding filling for turnovers and other savory pastries.

1 pound (454 g) coarsely chopped venison* (or regular ground venison)
2 teaspoons (30 ml) vegetable oil
1 medium onion, diced
1 green bell pepper, diced
3 cloves garlic, minced
1 can (16 ounces/454 g) whole tomatoes, drained
1 teaspoon (5 ml) paprika
½ teaspoon (2.5 ml) dried oregano leaves
½ teaspoon (2.5 ml) ground cumin
½ cup (120 ml/60 g) chopped pimiento-stuffed Spanish green olives
2 tablespoons (30 ml) chopped raisins, chopped before measuring
2 tablespoons (30 ml) red wine vinegar

In large skillet, cook venison in oil over medium heat until no longer pink, stirring frequently to break up. Add onion, bell pepper and garlic; cook, stirring occasionally, until vegetables are tender-crisp, about 5 minutes. Drain and discard excess grease; transfer venison mixture to slow cooker. Add tomatoes, crushing them with your hands as you add them to the slow cooker. Add remaining ingredients; stir well. Cover and cook on low for 4 hours, or on high for 2 hours; mixture can cook up to 6 hours on low.

GOOSE-STUFFED PEPPERS

4 servings
Prep: 30 minutes
Cooking: 6 hours on low, or 3 hours on high
Slow cooker: Standard

If you've got a shot-up goose, or some assorted goose parts that you're not sure how to prepare, try this tasty and colorful dish. Be sure to carefully pick out any shot, or bone fragments, from the meat before chopping it.

¾ pound (340 g) boneless, skinless goose meat
Half of a small onion
1 cup (235 ml/160 g) cooked rice (brown, white or wild)
½ cup (120 ml) seasoned bread crumbs
1 tablespoon (15 ml) Worcestershire sauce
½ teaspoon (2.5 ml) salt
1 egg, lightly beaten
4 whole red, green or yellow bell peppers
2 cans (14½ ounces/411 g) diced tomatoes, undrained
3 tablespoons (45 ml) packed brown sugar
A few dashes of Tabasco

Cut goose meat into 1-inch (2.5 cm) cubes. Chop in food processor to hamburger consistency; you could also use a meat grinder, running meat through twice. Transfer meat to mixing bowl. Add onion to food processor; chop medium-fine. Add rice, bread crumbs, Worcestershire sauce, salt and egg to mixing bowl. Mix well with a wooden spoon or your hands.

Cut tops off peppers. Pull out and discard core and any seedy ribs without breaking the peppers, which must remain intact. Divide meat mixture evenly between peppers, packing in fairly firmly and mounding the top. Place peppers upright in slow cooker; if they threaten to fall over, prop them up with foil balls (this may be necessary in a large slow cooker). In same mixing bowl, stir together tomatoes and their juices, brown sugar and Tabasco. Pour tomato mixture over and around peppers. Cover slow cooker; cook on low for 6 hours, or on high for 3 hours. Spoon sauce from slow cooker over peppers when serving.

VENISON-STUFFED PEPPERS
Follow directions above, substituting ¾ pound (340 g) ground venison for the goose.

SWEET AND SOUR MEATBALLS

4 to 6 main-dish servings, or 8 to 10 appetizer servings
Prep: 30 minutes, plus 15 minutes before final cooking on high
Cooking: 3 hours on low, followed by 1¼ hours on high
Slow cooker: Standard

For a main course, serve with hot white rice and canned chow mein noodles. For a party appetizer, make smaller meatballs and have a jar of cocktail forks next to the slow cooker.

1 egg
2 tablespoons (30 ml) flour
½ teaspoon (2.5 ml) salt
1½ pounds (680 g) ground venison
Half of a small onion, grated or
 finely minced
1 to 2 tablespoons (15 to 30 ml)
 vegetable oil, as needed
1½ cups (350 ml) pineapple juice
¼ cup (60 ml) rice vinegar or cider vinegar

¼ cup (60 ml/55 g) packed brown sugar
3 tablespoons (45 ml/25 g) cornstarch
2 tablespoons (30 ml) soy sauce
2 tablespoons (30 ml) ketchup
1 teaspoon (5 ml) minced fresh gingerroot
1 green or red bell pepper (or a mix),
 cut into ½ x 1½-inch
 (1.25 x 4 cm) strips
4 ounces (110 g) fresh snow pea pods,
 cut in half crosswise

In mixing bowl, blend together egg, flour and salt with a fork. Add venison and onion; mix gently but thoroughly with your hands. Shape into meatballs (walnut-sized for a main dish, or about 1 inch/2.5 cm for appetizers). Heat 1 tablespoon (15 ml) of the oil in large skillet over medium heat until shimmering. Add meatballs in a single layer and brown on all sides; you may need to brown in two batches and may need the additional oil. Transfer browned meatballs to slow cooker.

In saucepan, combine pineapple juice, vinegar, brown sugar, cornstarch, soy sauce, ketchup and gingerroot; mix well. Cook over medium heat, stirring frequently, until sauce comes to a boil and thickens somewhat. Pour sauce over meatballs in slow cooker. Cover and cook on low for 3 hours. Increase heat to high. Gently stir in bell pepper strips and pea pods; re-cover and cook for 1¼ hours longer.

SWEET AND SOUR MEATBALLS WITH GOOSE OR DUCK
Follow recipe above, except you'll be chopping your own goose or duck to replace the venison. You'll need 1 pound (454 g) boneless, skinless goose or duck, and ½ pound (225 g) boneless pork chops with a bit of fat. Cut the waterfowl and pork into 1-inch (2.5 cm) cubes, then chop to hamburger consistency. Proceed as directed above.

Lasagna-Style Layered Casserole

6 servings
Prep: 30 minutes
Cooking: 5 1/2 hours on low, or 2 1/2 hours on high
Slow cooker: Standard or Large

Traditional lasagna noodles don't fit very well in the slow cooker! Here's a casserole that offers the same goodness as regular lasagna, but is developed especially for the slow cooker. If you like, substitute uncooked venison sausage (uncased if links) for the ground venison.

6 ounces (170 g) uncooked mini lasagna noodles or other smaller,
  wavy-edged noodles
1 pound (454 g) ground venison
1 teaspoon (5 ml) vegetable oil
1 jar (26 ounces/737 g) marinara sauce or other tomato-based pasta sauce
1 pound (454 g) ricotta cheese (reduced-fat works fine)
2 cups (8 ounces/230 g/475 ml) shredded mozzarella cheese
1/4 cup (60 ml) water
1/4 cup (30 g/60 ml) shredded Parmesan cheese

In a large pot of boiling water, cook noodles until not quite tender; they should still be fairly firm in the middle (the noodles will get additional cooking in the slow cooker). Drain and rinse with cold running water, then leave in colander to continue draining while you prepare sauce. In medium saucepan, cook venison in oil over medium heat until no longer pink, stirring frequently to break up. Drain and discard excess fat. Add marinara sauce to saucepan; cook, stirring occasionally, for about 5 minutes. Remove from heat.

Spray inside of slow cooker with nonstick spray. Spread a thin layer of the meat-sauce mixture in bottom of slow cooker (use a bit less than one-quarter of the sauce for this layer). Top with one-third of the noodles. Spoon one-third of the ricotta cheese over the noodles. Top with one-third of the remaining meat-sauce mixture. Scatter one-third of the mozzarella cheese over the meat sauce. Repeat layers twice, ending with mozzarella cheese. Add water to saucepan in which sauce was cooked; swirl around, then pour water into slow cooker. Sprinkle Parmesan cheese evenly over the top of the casserole. Cover and cook on low for 5 1/2 hours, or on high for 2 1/2 hours; cheese should be melted and mixture should be bubbling around the edges.

ITALIAN VENISON STEW

6 servings
Prep: 30 minutes
Cooking: 7½ hours on low, or 4 hours on high (can cook up to 9 hours on low)
Slow cooker: Standard or Large

Serve this delicious stew with buttered noodles, a loaf of bread and a big green salad.

2-pound (900-g) venison roast, well trimmed before weighing
½ cup (120 ml/70 g) all-purpose flour
½ teaspoon (2.5 ml) salt
½ teaspoon (2.5 ml) paprika
3 tablespoons (45 ml) olive oil, divided
8 ounces (225 g) fresh green beans
15 to 20 pearl onions, peeled*
3 cloves garlic, coarsely chopped
1 cup Chianti (235 ml) or other dry red wine
1 can (14½ ounces/411 g) Italian-seasoned stewed tomatoes, undrained
1 can (15 ounces/425 g) garbanzo beans, drained and rinsed
4 ounces (115 g) pitted olives such as Kalamata
1 teaspoon (5 ml) dried Italian herb blend

Rinse roast and pat dry. Cut into 1½-inch (4-cm) cubes, trimming away any silverskin or fat. In plastic food-storage bag, combine flour, salt and paprika; close bag and shake to combine. Add venison; shake to coat.

In Dutch oven, heat half of the oil over medium-high heat until shimmering. Remove half of the floured venison cubes from bag, shaking off excess flour; add to Dutch oven and brown on all sides. While venison is browning, trim green beans and cut into 1½-inch (4-cm) lengths; add to slow cooker. Use tongs to transfer browned venison to slow cooker; brown remaining venison in remaining oil. Transfer second batch of browned venison to slow cooker. Add onions to Dutch oven; cook until they begin to color, 3 to 5 minutes, stirring several times. Add garlic; cook for about a minute, stirring frequently. Add wine, stirring to loosen any browned bits. Cook for about 3 minutes, then pour into slow cooker. Add tomatoes with their juices, drained garbanzo beans and olives; stir to combine. Cover and cook on low for 7½ hours, or on high for 4 hours; the stew can cook up to 9 hours on low. Just before serving, stir dried herbs into stew and let stand for about 5 minutes.

*To peel pearl onions: Drop them into a pot of rapidly boiling water. Boil for one minute, then drain and rinse with cold water. Trim off the root ends; the skins should slip off easily.

VENISON-MUSHROOM STROGANOFF

5 or 6 servings
Prep: Under 30 minutes; requires a bit of additional prep shortly before serving
Cooking: 7 to 8 hours on low, or 3½ to 4 hours on high, plus 15 to 30 minutes on
*   high shortly before serving*
Slow cooker: Standard

1½ pounds (680 g) boneless venison
   round steak
1 tablespoon (15 ml) vegetable oil, approx.
⅓ cup (80 ml) dry sherry
⅓ cup (80 ml) water
3 sprigs fresh parsley
2 cloves garlic
8 ounces (225 g) fresh mushrooms, sliced
1 cup (235 ml/140 g) frozen
   pearl onions, thawed

1 can (10½ ounces/298 g)
   beef consommé
½ teaspoon (2.5 ml) dried thyme leaves
½ teaspoon (2.5 ml) salt
¼ teaspoon (1.25 ml) pepper
1 cup (235 ml/227 g) sour cream
   (reduced-fat works fine)
⅓ cup (80 ml/45 g) all-purpose flour
Hot cooked noodles or rice

Cut venison into 1-inch (2.5-cm) cubes. In large skillet, heat oil over medium-high heat until shimmering. Add half of the venison and brown well on all sides. Transfer browned venison to slow cooker with slotted spoon. Brown remaining venison, adding additional oil if necessary; transfer to slow cooker. Add sherry and water to skillet with drippings and cook over medium heat, stirring to scrape up browned bits, for about a minute. Pour into slow cooker.

While venison is browning, chop together parsley leaves and garlic (discard parsley stems). Add parsley mixture, mushrooms, onions, consommé, thyme, salt and pepper to slow cooker; stir well. Cover and cook until venison is tender, 7 to 8 hours on low or 3½ to 4 hours on high (if you're at home, stir the mixture once or twice during cooking, replacing the lid as quickly as possible).

At end of cooking time, stir together sour cream and flour in small mixing bowl. Scoop out about 1 cup (235 ml) of hot liquid from slow cooker; stir into sour cream mixture and blend well with a fork. Increase slow cooker to high if necessary. Add sour cream mixture to slow cooker; re-cover. Cook for 15 to 30 minutes longer or until sauce thickens and bubbles, stirring once or twice. Serve over noodles or rice.

 ADVANCE PREPARATION AND COOKING TIME

When you brown meats and heat the liquid just before adding them to the slow cooker (as with the Venison-Mushroom Stroganoff), the food is already warm when you start timing, so you get a jump-start on cooking.

To save time in the morning, you can brown the meat and prepare the cooking liquid the night before, then keep the ingredients in separate containers in the refrigerator until the next day. However, the ingredients will be at a much lower temperature than if the prep was done just prior to cooking; it will take the slow cooker a while to warm them up to the temperature they would have been the way the recipe is written. If a recipe method calls for a "warm start" and you will be starting with cold ingredients instead, add 60 to 90 minutes cooking time if cooking on low, or 45 minutes if cooking on high.

PEPPER AND VENISON GOULASH

5 or 6 servings
Prep: 30 minutes, plus a bit of additional prep shortly before serving
Cooking: 9 hours on low, or 5 hours on high (can cook up to 10 hours on low)
Slow cooker: Standard

This dish gets flavor from three types of peppers: sweet green bell peppers, paprika (which is made of dried red peppers) and black pepper.

2 pounds (900 g) venison round steak
½ cup (120 ml/70 g) all-purpose flour
2 teaspoons (10 ml) dry mustard powder
2 tablespoon (30 ml) vegetable oil, divided
1 small onion, diced
1 or 2 cloves garlic, minced
2 green bell peppers, cut into 1/4-x-2-inch
   (6 mm x 5 cm) strips
1 can (14½ ounces/411 g)
   diced tomatoes, undrained
1 tablespoon (15 ml) paprika,
   preferably Hungarian

2 teaspoons (10 ml) sugar
1½ teaspoons (7.5 ml) salt
½ teaspoon (2.5 ml) black pepper,
   preferably freshly ground
½ teaspoon (2.5 ml) caraway seed,
   optional
¼ teaspoon (1.25 ml) nutmeg
1 cup (235 ml/227 g) sour cream
½ teaspoon (2.5 ml) dried thyme leaves
Hot cooked noodles

Pat venison dry; cut into finger-width strips about 2 inches (5 cm) long. In plastic food-storage bag, combine flour and dry mustard; close bag and shake to combine. Add venison; shake to coat. In large skillet, heat half of the oil over medium heat until shimmering. Add half of the floured venison; brown on all sides. Transfer venison to slow cooker; repeat with remaining venison and oil. Add onion, garlic, bell peppers, tomatoes and their juices, paprika, sugar, salt, black pepper, caraway seed and nutmeg to slow cooker; stir well. Cover and cook on low for 9 hours, or on high for 5 hours; stew can cook up to 10 hours on low. About 15 minutes before serving, stir in sour cream and thyme; re-cover and cook until hot. Serve over hot buttered noodles.

VARIATION:

For more texture, don't add the bell pepper strips to the slow cooker with the browned meat and other ingredients. After the meat has cooked for 3 hours on low (or 1 hour on high), add pepper strips to meat mixture; stir well, re-cover and continue cooking for total time as directed.

FRENCH-STYLE STEAKS WITH WINE AND BRANDY

5 or 6 servings
Prep: 45 minutes
Cooking: 6 1/2 to 7 1/2 hours on low
Slow cooker: Standard

1/2 **pound (225 g) thick-sliced bacon**
1 **large yellow onion**
5 **carrots, sliced**
1 **can (14 1/2 ounces/411 g)**
    diced tomatoes, drained
2 **cloves garlic, sliced**
Leaves from 4 sprigs fresh parsley,
    chopped
1 1/2 **teaspoons (7.5 ml) crumbled dried**
    rosemary leaves
1 1/2 **teaspoons (7.5 ml) dried thyme leaves**

2 **bay leaves**
2 **strips orange zest (orange part only),**
    finely chopped
2 **pounds (900 g) boneless venison**
    round steaks, 1/2 inch (1.25 cm) thick
Salt and pepper
1/2 **cup (120 ml) brandy**
2 **cups (475 ml) dry red wine**
1 **tablespoon (15 ml) Dijon mustard**

Cut bacon into 1/2-inch (1.25 cm) pieces. In large skillet, cook bacon over medium heat until not quite crisp. Transfer with slotted spoon to slow cooker; reserve drippings in skillet. Cut onion in half from top to bottom, then slice each half into vertical wedges about 1/4 inch (6 mm) thick. Add carrots, onion and tomatoes to slow cooker (do not stir). Sprinkle garlic, parsley, rosemary, thyme, bay leaves and orange zest over vegetables. Cut venison steaks into 2- to 3-inch (5 to 7.5 cm) pieces; sprinkle with salt and pepper. Brown in reserved bacon drippings over medium-high heat (you may have to brown in two batches). Arrange venison pieces over vegetables in slow cooker.

In saucepan, heat brandy over medium heat until just hot. Remove from heat. Following information in sidebar on page 53, carefully ignite brandy and allow to burn until flames die completely. Add wine to brandy. Cook over medium-high heat until liquid has reduced to about 1 1/3 cups (320 ml); take care, as the wine may ignite during cooking. Stir mustard into wine mixture. Pour hot wine mixture around venison in slow cooker. Cover and cook on low until tender, 6 1/2 to 7 1/2 hours. Discard bay leaves before serving. The sauce, although thin, is delicious with the vegetables and meat. If you prefer a thicker sauce, thicken as described in the sidebar on page 82.

Note: The hot wine mixture helps bring the food up to cooking temperature quickly. If you prepare the ingredients the night before and refrigerate them, the wine will be cold and the starting temperature will be lower, so the cooking time needs to be increased by about an hour.

SWEET AND SAVORY ROUND STEAKS

4 servings
Prep: 15 minutes
Cooking: 7 to 8 hours on low
Slow cooker: Standard

I like to serve this with cooked noodles, but mashed potatoes or rice would also work well. A side dish of broccoli or carrots adds color and nutrition.

1½ pounds (680 g) boneless venison,
   elk or moose round steaks,
   about 1 inch (2.5 cm) thick
Salt and pepper
All-purpose flour for dredging
2 tablespoons (30 ml) vegetable oil
⅓ cup (80 ml) beef broth or
   venison stock (page 27)

Half of a small onion, finely diced
3 tablespoons (45 ml)
   packed brown sugar
¼ cup (60 ml) ketchup
Dried basil leaves
1 tablespoon (15 g/15 ml) butter, cut up

Cut steak into 8 equal-sized pieces. Pound with meat mallet to ½ inch (1.25 cm) thickness. Sprinkle with salt and pepper; dredge in flour, shaking off excess. Heat oil in large skillet over medium-high heat. Add floured steaks; brown nicely on both sides. Meanwhile, spray inside of slow cooker with nonstick spray; add beef broth. Transfer browned steaks to slow cooker, tucking together to keep in a single layer. Sprinkle onion, then brown sugar, evenly over steaks. Distribute ketchup evenly over steaks in small dollops. Sprinkle basil generously over steaks. Dot with butter. Cover and cook on low until very tender, 7 to 8 hours. Serve steaks with juices from slow cooker.

☞ FLAMING LIQUOR ☜

When brandy and other hard liquor is used in cooking, it's often desirable to "flame" the liquor before using it in cooking liquid. Flaming burns off much of the alcohol, resulting in a smoother, mellower taste. Heat the liquor in a saucepan over low heat until just warm, then remove from heat. Using a long-handled match, ignite the fumes by holding the lit match over the saucepan at the edge. Here are some safety tips:• Roll up any long sleeves before starting; tie back long hair.• Never hold the match in a way that puts your hand over the saucepan (for extra safety, hold the match with a tongs when placing it over the saucepan).• Don't let flames burn underneath a vent hood; grease in the hood filter could ignite.• Let the flames die completely before adding anything or stirring the contents. Even after the flames have died, watch out for re-ignition when the pan is moved.

Southwestern Venison Stew

6 servings
Prep: 15 minutes
Cooking: 8 to 9 hours on low, or 4 to 4¹/₂ hours on high (can cook up to 10 hours on low)
Slow cooker: Standard or Large

I prefer yellow hominy in this stew, but white hominy works fine if that's what you can find. For the beer, I like to use Negra Modelo, a dark Mexican ale.

1¹/₂ to 2 pounds (680 to 900 g) boneless venison stew meat
2 tablespoons (30 ml) chili powder blend
1 teaspoon (5 ml) ground cumin
³/₄ teaspoon (3.75 ml) garlic salt or plain salt
1 tablespoon (15 ml) vegetable oil
1 medium onion, diced
1 red bell pepper, cut into ³/₄-inch (2-cm) cubes
1 cup (235 ml) dark beer

2 tablespoons (30 ml) tomato paste
1 tablespoon (15 ml) cornmeal
1 tablespoon (15 ml) red wine vinegar
1 can (15¹/₂ ounces/439 g) hominy,* drained and rinsed
1 can (4¹/₂ ounces/127 g) chopped green chile peppers
1 can (15 ounces/425 g) pinto beans, drained and rinsed
¹/₄ cup (60 ml) chopped fresh cilantro
1 lime, cut into wedges

Cut venison into cubes that are approximately 1¹/₂ inches (3.75 cm). Sprinkle with chili powder blend, cumin and salt, tossing with your hands to coat evenly. In large skillet, heat oil over medium-high heat until shimmering. Add half of the venison and brown on all sides; if the oil starts smoking, reduce heat slightly. Transfer venison with slotted spoon to slow cooker. Brown remaining venison; transfer to slow cooker.

Add onion and bell pepper to skillet; cook for about 5 minutes, stirring frequently. Transfer vegetables to slow cooker. Add beer to skillet, stirring to loosen any browned bits. Cook over medium-high heat until beer just comes to a boil. Add tomato paste, cornmeal and vinegar to skillet, stirring to blend, then pour into slow cooker. Add hominy, chiles and beans to slow cooker. Cover and cook until venison is tender, 8 to 9 hours on low or 4 to 4¹/₂ hours on high; stew can cook up to 10 hours on low. Just before serving, scatter cilantro over stew. Serve with lime wedges.

*Hominy, which is also called posole or pozole, is dried corn kernels that have been soaked in a special mixture that swells the kernels; the hull is removed after soaking. Hominy has a pleasantly chewy texture and a rich corn taste. Look for hominy with the canned vegetables.

SWEET AND TANGY ASIAN-STYLE VENISON

4 servings
Prep: 15 minutes, plus a bit of additional prep shortly before serving
Cooking: 6 hours on low, or 3 hours on high (can cook up to 7 hours on low),
  plus 15 minutes on high shortly before serving
Slow cooker: Standard

Tender venison strips are bathed in a sweet-tangy Asian-influenced sauce … perfect with steamed white rice.

1 medium onion, cut in half from top to bottom and sliced
½ cup (120 ml) light soy sauce
1 cup (235 ml) chicken broth
3 tablespoons (45 ml) hoisin sauce*
3 tablespoons (45 ml) packed brown sugar
2 teaspoons (10 ml) minced fresh gingerroot
½ teaspoon (2.5 ml) hot red pepper flakes
1 pound (454 g) venison roast or steaks, sliced thinly across the grain
¼ cup (60 ml/30 g) cornstarch
¼ cup (60 ml) dry sherry
4 green onions, sliced (white and green parts)
1 tablespoon (15 ml) sesame seeds

In slow cooker, combine onion, soy sauce, broth, hoisin sauce, brown sugar, gingerroot and pepper flakes; stir to blend. In plastic food-storage bag, combine thinly sliced venison and cornstarch; shake to coat. Remove venison from bag, shaking off excess cornstarch. Place venison into slow cooker with sauce mixture, pushing venison into sauce mixture to coat (do not stir). Sprinkle sherry over venison. Cover and cook on low for 6 hours, or on high for 3 hours; venison can cook up to 7 hours on low.

When venison has cooked the proper amount of time, increase heat to high if necessary. Sprinkle green onion over venison; re-cover and cook for 15 minutes longer. Sprinkle with sesame seeds just before serving.

*Hoisin sauce is a sweet, dark, thick sauce used in Chinese cooking. Look for it in the Asian section of the supermarket, or at a specialty Asian market.

Boar Chops 'n Kraut

6 servings
Prep: 30 minutes
Cooking: 7 to 8 hours on low
Slow cooker: Large (see note for standard-sized slow cooker)

Sauerkraut from the deli case (in plastic bags) has a fresher taste than canned or jarred sauerkraut, and is preferred for this dish. Serve this with hot buttered noodles and a vegetable side dish.

1 bag (2 pounds/907 g) sauerkraut, drained
3 slices bacon, diced
6 thick wild boar chops, 6 to 8 ounces (175 to 225 g) each
Salt and pepper
2 medium onions, chopped
½ cup (120 ml) dry white wine or chicken broth
3 tablespoons (45 ml) packed brown sugar
1 tablespoon (15 ml) Dijon mustard
2 medium apples, peeled and diced
2 cloves garlic, crushed
8 whole black peppercorns, crushed

Rinse sauerkraut in strainer; set aside to drain while you prepare chops. In large skillet, cook bacon over medium heat until beginning to crisp. Drain all but about 1 tablespoon (15 ml) bacon grease. Pat chops dry; season lightly with salt and pepper. Add to skillet and brown on one side. Turn chops; add onion to skillet and cook until chops are browned on second side. When chops are almost browned, transfer drained sauerkraut to slow cooker. Stir in wine, brown sugar, mustard, apples, garlic and peppercorns. When chops are browned, place on top of sauerkraut, overlapping as little as possible and placing the thicker edges to the outside of the slow cooker. Spoon bacon and onions remaining in skillet over chops. Cover slow cooker. Cook on low until chops are tender, 7 to 8 hours.

Note: For a standard-sized slow cooker, use 4 chops instead of 6, but use the full amount of sauerkraut and other ingredients. Arrange the 4 chops on top of the sauerkraut as directed, overlapping as little as possible and placing the thicker edges to the outside of the slow cooker. Cook as directed. You'll have extra sauerkraut (unless someone really loves it!), but the proportions are good as written and don't need to be altered for the smaller number of chops.

ELK SWISS STEAK

6 servings
Prep: 15 minutes
Cooking: 8 to 9 hours on low, or 4 to 4¼ hours on high (can cook up to 10 hours on low)
Slow cooker: Standard or Large

If you aren't fortunate enough to have elk in your freezer, substitute venison, antelope or moose. The best steaks for this dish are from the round or rump, preferably about ¾ inch (2 cm) thick. Serve this with hot buttered noodles or mashed potatoes, to catch all the savory gravy.

1½ to 2 pounds (680 to 900 g) boneless elk steak
1 teaspoon (5 ml) dry mustard powder
Salt and pepper
¼ cup (60 ml/35 g) all-purpose flour
2 tablespoons (30 ml) vegetable oil
2 small onions, sliced
1 can (14½ ounces/411 g) whole tomatoes, undrained
1 tablespoon (15 ml) packed brown sugar
1 envelope (generally about 1 ounce/28 g, depending on brand) brown gravy mix
1 red or green bell pepper, cut into strips

Cut steaks into 6 equal pieces. Sprinkle evenly with mustard powder, and salt and pepper to taste; pound seasonings in lightly with meat mallet or the edge of a plate. Place flour in plastic food-storage bag. Add steaks, 1 or 2 at a time, and shake to coat; shake off excess flour. In large skillet, heat oil over medium heat until shimmering. Add steaks in a single layer; brown on both sides. While steaks are browning, scatter onions in bottom of slow cooker. Top with browned steaks.

In medium mixing bowl, stir together tomatoes and their juices, sugar and gravy mix, breaking tomatoes into slightly smaller pieces. Pour tomato mixture over steaks. Top with bell peppers. Cover and cook until steaks are tender, 8 to 9 hours on low or 4 to 4¼ hours on high; steaks can cook up to 10 hours on low.

TO BROWN, OR NOT TO BROWN

While you certainly can put roasts, stew meat and steaks into the slow cooker without browning them first, I generally recommend this extra step, which adds both flavor and color to the finished dish and gives the meat a better appearance. After browning the meat, I usually deglaze the skillet with some of the liquid used in the recipe; this captures the browned bits that remain behind in the skillet, and adds depth to the sauce.

Ground meat that's used "loose" in a dish (such as chili, casseroles or sloppy Joes) should always be thoroughly cooked by browning before going into the slow cooker; it's a good idea to brown meatballs as well. Uncooked ground meat may harbor food-borne bacteria, and cooking to a temperature of 160°F (71°C) kills bacteria such as E. coli. Browning also allows you to remove any excess fat, which otherwise would be trapped in the dish. Finally, it adds delicious flavor to the finished dish.

Small game and gamebirds can also be browned before going into the slow cooker, although this is not as important as it is with red meat.

STUFFED VENISON ROLLS

6 servings
Prep: 30 minutes
Cooking: 8 to 9 hours on low, or 4 to 4½ hours on high
Slow cooker: Standard

For a nice twist, use half dry sherry and half beef broth for the broth called for in the recipe.

1½ pounds (680 g)venison round steak, about ½ inch (1.25 cm) thick
2 slices bacon, diced
¼ cup (60 ml) diced onion
2 to 3 ounces (60 to 90 g) fresh mushrooms, sliced
½ cup (120 ml) water
¾ cup (180 ml) instant (finely textured) stuffing mix such as Stovetop Stuffing
1 can (10¾ ounces/305 g) condensed cream of mushroom soup
⅔ cup (160 ml) beef broth
You'll also need several lengths of heavy kitchen string

Cut steak into 6 equal portions. Pound each between sheets of plastic wrap until about ¼ inch (6 mm) thick; set aside. In large skillet, cook bacon over medium heat, stirring frequently, until beginning to crisp. Drain and discard all but about 2 teaspoons (10 ml) drippings. Add onion and mushrooms to skillet; continue cooking until vegetables are just tender. Add water; heat until just boiling. Remove from heat; stir in stuffing mix and set aside to cool slightly. Divide stuffing mixture evenly between pounded steak; roll up and secure with kitchen string. In slow cooker, combine soup and broth, stirring until blended. Add stuffed steaks, nestling them snugly in a single layer; if any stuffing has come out of the rolls or you have a bit left over, distribute it around the edges of the rolls. Cover and cook on low until meat is tender, 8 to 9 hours on low or 4 to 4½ hours on high. Serve rolls with sauce from slow cooker.

VARIATION: STUFFED VENISON ROLLS WITH STUFFING ON THE SIDE

Pound venison as directed above; set aside. For the stuffing, use a large skillet. Cook 4 slices diced bacon as directed; drain all but 1 tablespoon (15 ml) of the drippings. Add 1 medium onion, diced, and 8 ounces (225 g) sliced mushrooms to skillet; cook until tender. Add 1½ cups (350 ml) water to skillet; heat until just boiling. Remove from heat; stir in 2½ cups (590 ml/140 g) stuffing mix. Stuff each steak with about ¼ cup (60 ml) of the cooled stuffing mix; roll and tie as directed. Spoon remaining stuffing into a greased casserole; cover and refrigerate. Continue with recipe as directed. About 45 minutes before you plan to serve the venison rolls, place covered casserole in preheated 350°F (175°C) oven. Bake for 30 minutes, then remove cover and bake for 15 minutes longer. Serve stuffing with venison rolls and sauce.

Classic Venison Pot Roast

6 to 8 servings
Prep: 30 minutes, plus 15 minutes shortly before serving
Cooking: 8 1/2 to 9 1/2 hours on low, or 4 1/2 to 5 hours on high (can cook up to 10 hours
  on low); requires 15 minutes stovetop cooking shortly before serving
Slow cooker: Large

Here's a great way to cook a less-tender venison cut. Browning the meat before cooking produces a rich, flavorful gravy. Serve this with mashed potatoes, or with sturdy egg noodles.

5-pound (2.3 kg) boneless venison
   chuck roast, tied if necessary
Salt and pepper
1 tablespoon (15 ml) vegetable oil,
   or a bit more as needed
2 medium onions, coarsely chopped
3 cloves garlic, chopped
4 carrots, cut into 2-inch (5 cm) pieces
2 ribs celery, cut into 2-inch (5 cm) pieces

2 bay leaves
1 cup (235 ml) dry red wine
1 can (28 ounces/794 g)
   plum tomatoes, undrained
3 cups (690 ml) beef broth or
   venison stock (page 27)
1 tablespoon (15 ml) dried herb blend
2 tablespoons (30 ml) cornstarch
3/4 cup (180 ml) cold water

Rinse roast and pat dry with paper towels. Season generously with salt and pepper. In Dutch oven, heat oil over medium-high heat until shimmering. Add roast, and brown well on all sides; if the oil starts smoking, reduce heat slightly. Transfer roast to slow cooker; set aside.

Add onion and garlic to Dutch oven (add a bit more oil if necessary). Cook until golden, stirring frequently. While onion cooks, arrange carrots, celery and bay leaves around roast in slow cooker. When onions are golden, add wine to Dutch oven, stirring to loosen any browned bits. Cook until wine has reduced by about half. Add tomatoes and their juices, along with broth and herbs, to Dutch oven; stir to mix and pour into slow cooker. Cover and cook until roast is tender, 8 1/2 to 9 1/2 hours on low or 4 1/2 to 5 hours on high; roast can cook up to 10 hours on low.

When roast is tender, transfer roast, carrots and celery to serving platter; discard bay leaves. Tent roast loosely with foil. Use a large spoon to skim fat from surface of mixture in slow cooker. Carefully ladle mixture from slow cooker into blender or food processor, and purée until smooth. Pour mixture into saucepan; heat over medium-high heat until just boiling. In mixing cup, blend cornstarch and cold water. Add half of the cornstarch mixture to the saucepan and cook, stirring constantly, until bubbly. Add additional cornstarch slurry as needed and continue to cook until gravy is desired thickness. Taste for seasoning and adjust if necessary. Serve gravy with roast and vegetables.

VEGETABLES AND THE SLOW COOKER

Root vegetables such as carrots, potatoes and parsnips take longer to become tender in a slow cooker than does meat. Older recipes for the slow cooker may direct you to place these vegetables on the bottom, because with older slow cookers, that's where the heat was. Modern slow cookers have heating elements in the sides, however, so this advice no longer applies. If you're cooking a pot roast or other large cut, place the roast in the cooker, then tuck the vegetables around the sides, where they'll get more heat. Tender vegetables such as zucchini are best if added in the last 30 minutes of cooking.

HERB AND GARLIC GAME ROAST FOR A CROWD

10 to 12 servings
Prep: 15 minutes, plus 15 minutes shortly before serving
Cooking: 6 to 7 hours on low, plus 15 minutes additional cooking just before serving
Slow cooker: Medium roaster

If you like, you can prepare the roast the day before you plan to serve it. Slice the meat and return it to the juice; cover and refrigerate until an hour before you plan to serve it. An hour before serving, heat roaster to 200°F (93°C). Add meat and juice to roaster, and cook until hot.

5-pound (2.3 kg) elk, moose or venison roast
6 cloves garlic, each cut into several slivers
2 tablespoons (30 ml) olive oil or vegetable oil
Salt and pepper
½ cup (125 ml) chopped fresh parsley
½ cup (125 ml) chopped fresh basil
2 tablespoons (30 ml) chopped fresh oregano, or 1 tablespoon (15 ml) dried oregano leaves
2 to 3 cups (470 to 690 ml) beef broth or venison stock (page 27), or as needed

Preheat roaster to 175°F (80°C). While roaster is heating, rinse roast and pat dry with paper towels. With sharp paring knife, pierce deep slits into roast; insert a garlic sliver into each slit. Rub roast with oil; sprinkle all sides with salt and pepper to taste. In mixing bowl, stir together parsley, basil and oregano. Place roast on rack in roaster. Sprinkle herb mixture over roast, patting gently. Add enough broth to come about an inch (2.5 cm) up the sides of the roaster. Cover and cook for 6 to 7 hours, or until roast is tender. Transfer roast to cutting board; let stand for about 10 minutes. Slice roast thinly, returning slices to roaster. Let sliced meat sit in roaster for at least 15 minutes to marinate in the juices (the meat can sit in the roaster for an hour or longer at this point).

 GETTING DEPTH OF FLAVOR WITH SLOW-COOKED DISHES

Roasts and stews cooked in the slow cooker sometimes seem to be rather one-dimensional. This is partly because the liquid doesn't get concentrated as it does in many other types of cooking, and also because meat doesn't brown during slow cooking as it does during oven roasting. One way to add additional depth of flavor is to brown meats, where appropriate, before adding them to the slow cooker. This extra step takes a bit of time, but adds richness to the finished dish.

To capture the maximum flavor from browning, use the liquid from the recipe to deglaze the pan in which the meat was browned, then add it to the slow cooker. This way, all the good, browned flavor is transferred to the dish.

SAVORY BOAR ROAST WITH APPLES

5 or 6 servings
Prep: 15 minutes
Cooking: 7 to 8 hours on low, or 3 to 3½ hours on high
Slow cooker: Standard

Cooking time depends on the tenderness of the boar roast, and the specific cut. This method creates a delicious, dark brown gravy; the longer the roast cooks, the darker and richer the gravy will be. Serve the roast—and the savory gravy—with mashed white-and-sweet potatoes, and a green vegetable.

2½- to 3-pound (1.125 to 1.5 kg) wild boar roast, preferably boneless
    (if using bone-in, choose the larger roast size)
3 cloves garlic, each cut into several slivers
Salt and pepper
2 tablespoons (30 ml) vegetable oil
1 cup (235 ml) apple juice
3 tablespoons (45 ml) packed brown sugar
2 tablespoons (30 ml) all-purpose flour
1 tablespoon (15 ml) Dijon mustard
2 teaspoons (10 ml) minced fresh gingerroot
¼ teaspoon (1.25 ml) hot red pepper flakes, optional
1 cup (235 ml/about 2½ ounces/70 g) dried apple slices

Rinse roast and pat dry with paper towels. With sharp paring knife, pierce deep slits into roast; insert a garlic sliver into each slit. Season roast generously with salt and pepper. In large pot, heat oil over medium heat until shimmering. Add roast, and brown on all sides. While roast is browning, combine apple juice, brown sugar, flour, mustard, gingerroot and pepper flakes in measuring cup or mixing bowl; stir to blend. When roast is browned, transfer to slow cooker. Top with apple slices; pour apple-juice mixture over roast. Cover and cook until roast is tender, 7 to 8 hours on low, or 3 to 3½ hours on high (if you're cooking on high, you may reduce the temperature to low after about 3½ hours on high, and continue cooking on low for an hour or two longer). Transfer roast to serving platter; let stand for 10 minutes before slicing. Skim fat from juices with a large spoon. Serve roast with apples and juices from slow cooker.

SIMPLE SAUERBRATEN

5 to 7 servings
Prep: 15 minutes, plus 15 minutes shortly before serving
Cooking: 8 to 9 hours on low (can cook up to 10 hours),
   plus 15 minutes on high shortly before serving
Slow cooker: Standard

Meat for sauerbraten is usually marinated for several days. This simpler version has the tangy-sweet flavor of sauerbraten—without all the fuss. If you prefer a smooth sauce, pass it through a wire-mesh strainer, pressing on the onions, before serving (I like the onions with the meat, so I leave them in the sauce even though it is less traditional).

2- to 3-pound (1 to 1.5 kg) venison roast, preferably from the rump or round
Salt and pepper
2 tablespoons (30 ml) vegetable oil
2 medium onions, sliced, divided into 2 portions
6 whole juniper berries, optional
6 whole cloves
1 bay leaf
A small square of cheesecloth and a piece of kitchen string
2 cups (475 ml) beef broth
1/3 cup (80 ml) red wine vinegar
1/4 cup (60 ml/55 g) packed brown sugar
10 gingersnaps (2 inch/5 cm diameter), finely crushed

Rinse roast, and pat dry with paper towels. Season generously with salt and pepper. In Dutch oven, heat oil over medium-high heat until shimmering. Add roast, and brown well on all sides; if the oil starts smoking, reduce heat slightly. While roast is browning, scatter half of the onions into slow cooker. Tie juniper berries, cloves and bay leaf together in cheesecloth; add spice bundle to slow cooker. When roast is browned, transfer to slow cooker. Add broth, vinegar and brown sugar to Dutch oven. Cook, stirring constantly, until sugar dissolves and mixture comes to a boil. Transfer broth mixture to slow cooker. Top roast with remaining onions. Cover slow cooker. Cook until tender, 8 to 9 hours on low; roast can cook up to 10 hours. When roast is tender and you're almost ready to serve, use two forks to transfer roast to serving platter. Discard spice bundle. Increase slow cooker to high. Stir gingersnaps into liquid mixture in slow cooker. Cover and cook until sauce thickens somewhat, about 15 minutes. Slice roast or break into large chunks, depending on cut and tenderness; serve with sauce (sauce may be strained if you like; see note above).

Apple Cider Roast

10 servings
Prep: 15 minutes
Cooking: 1 to 1½ hours on high
Slow cooker: Medium roaster

4-pound (1.8 kg) boneless venison roast from the loin, rump or round
2 tablespoons (30 g/30 ml) butter, softened
1 tablespoon (15 ml) Dijon mustard
2 tablespoons (30 ml) packed brown sugar
1 tablespoon (15 ml) cracked black pepper
1 teaspoon (5 ml) crumbled dried rosemary leaves
1 teaspoon (5 ml) kosher salt
1 large onion, sliced
1 cup (235 ml) apple juice
1 tablespoon (15 ml) juice from a jar of pickles

Preheat roaster to 325°F (164°C). While roaster is heating, rinse roast and pat dry with paper towels. In small bowl, blend together butter and mustard; spread over all sides of roast. In another small bowl, mix together sugar, pepper, rosemary and salt; sprinkle evenly over roast, patting into butter. Place roast on rack in roaster. Scatter onion slices over roast. Pour apple juice and pickle juice into roaster. Cover and cook at 325°F (164°C) until the roast is done to your preference (see chart below). Transfer roast to serving platter. Tent loosely with foil and let stand for 10 minutes before slicing.

 HOW TO DETERMINE DONENESS OF A VENISON ROAST

In most cases, the venison roasts you'll be preparing in the slow cooker are those that require long, slow cooking in a moist environment—braising—to become tender; pot roast is a good example of this. To check for doneness of these cuts, probe the roast with a fork; it should feel tender. Electric countertop roasters, however, do an excellent job of cooking the naturally tender roasts from the loin, rump and round; as with oven roasting, doneness is generally judged by internal temperature of the meat. Tender venison roasts are best when they're still pink and juicy inside; if these roasts are cooked to well-done, they are likely to be tough and dry, since venison lacks the internal marbling of beef. This chart gives temperature ranges for tender venison roasts. To check the temperature, insert an instant-read thermometer into the center of the roast (avoid any bone).

DONENESS	°F	°C	DONENESS	°F	°C
Rare	130-135	54-57	Medium-well*	150-155	66-68
Medium-rare	135-140	57-60	Well-done*	155-160	68-71
Medium	140-145	60-63	*Not recommended for tender venison roasts, especially prime roasts from the loin*		

Venison Roast Braised with Grenadine

4 or 5 servings
Prep: 15 minutes
Cooking: 7 to 8 hours on low
Slow cooker: Standard

I was working with some Persian ingredients, and prepared a venison roast with pomegranate syrup. It was delicious: slightly sweet, with an interesting yet easy-to-love flavor. Because pomegranate syrup can be hard to find, I developed this recipe using grenadine syrup, which is similar and much easier to find; look for it at any liquor store, or with the bar mixes in a supermarket.

2-pound (1 kg) boneless venison rump roast
Salt and pepper
1 tablespoon (15 ml) olive oil

1 medium yellow onion
½ cup (120 ml) chicken broth
¼ cup (60 ml) grenadine syrup

Rinse roast and pat dry with paper towels. Season generously with salt and pepper. In Dutch oven, heat oil over medium-high heat until shimmering. Add roast and brown well on all sides; if the oil starts smoking, reduce heat slightly. While roast is browning, cut onion in half from top to bottom, then cut each half across the equator. Cut each quarter into ¼-inch-wide (6 mm) wedges from top to bottom (rather than half rings). Add onion wedges to Dutch oven with roast, and stir them around occasionally while roast is browning. In measuring cup, combine broth and grenadine.

When roast is nicely browned, transfer to slow cooker along with onions. Add broth mixture to Dutch oven, stirring to loosen any browned bits. Cook over medium heat for about a minute, then pour over roast in slow cooker. Cover and cook on low until roast is very tender, 7 to 8 hours. To serve, transfer roast to cutting board and let stand for a few minutes, then cut or break the roast apart into chunks. Place venison chunks in serving bowl; pour juices and onions from slow cooker over the top.

VARIATION: RABBIT BRAISED WITH GRENADINE

Follow recipe above, substituting 2½ pounds (1.125 kg) bone-in rabbit pieces for the venison roast. Cooking time should be 6 to 7 hours, depending on the age of the rabbit(s). To serve, simply pile the cooked pieces in a serving bowl; pour the juices and onion from the slow cooker over the pieces.

BRUNCH BREAD PUDDING WITH BACON, FRUIT AND NUTS: P. 10

PHEASANT AND NOODLE SOUP: P. 17

TACO SOUP: P. 24

TEXAS PRIDE CHILI: P. 31

BIG-GAME TACOS: P. 34

BLUE-PLATE SPECIAL: OPEN-FACED TURKEY SANDWICHES: P. 37

GOOSE-STUFFED PEPPERS: P. 46

SWEET AND SOUR MEATBALLS: P. 47

SWEET AND SAVORY ROUND STEAKS: P. 53

STUFFED VENISON ROLLS: P. 58

RABBIT WITH MUSTARD: P. 89

PHEASANT-STUFFED MANICOTTI: P. 98

ORANGE-SAUCED DUCK: P. 104

PARTY NACHOS WITH VENISON: P.111

SCALLOPED TWO-COLOR POTATOES: P. 117

HONEY-SWEET WILD BOAR RIBS

2 or 3 servings*
Prep: 15 minutes, plus about 15 minutes shortly before serving
Cooking: 7 to 9 hours on low, or 3 to 4 hours on high, plus 15 minutes stovetop cooking
Slow cooker: Standard*

Here are fall-off-the-bone-tender boar ribs that have a touch of sweetness to offset the rich boar meat. Cooking time will depend on the age—and tenderness—of the boar; when the ribs are done, the meat will have shrunk away from the bone at the tips and will pull away from the bone easily.

1 can (10½ ounces/298 g) beef broth
⅓ cup (80 ml) honey
¼ cup (60 ml) barbecue sauce
¼ cup (60 ml) maple syrup
3 tablespoons (45 ml) Dijon mustard
2 tablespoons (30 ml) soy sauce
Half of a small onion, minced
1 clove garlic, minced
2 to 3 pounds (1 to 1.5 kg) wild boar ribs, excess fat trimmed

Add broth, honey, barbecue sauce, syrup, mustard, soy sauce, onion and garlic to slow cooker; stir well. Cut ribs into 2- or 3-bone portions. Add to sauce in slow cooker, turning to coat. Cover slow cooker; cook on low for 7 to 9 hours (or 3 to 4 hours on high), until meat is very tender; rearrange the ribs in the sauce midway through cooking if possible. When meat is very tender, transfer to serving dish. Use a wide, shallow spoon (or a gravy separator) to remove fat from juices in slow cooker. Transfer juices to heavy saucepan. Cook over high heat until reduced by half. Serve ribs with reduced juices (if you like, arrange ribs on broiler pan and brush with reduced juices; broil for a few minutes to heat and crisp the ribs).

*For a larger batch, use a large slow cooker (or a medium roaster, preheated to 250°F/120°C; cooking time will be 3 to 4 hours) and double all ingredients.

 ENERGY USE AND THE SLOW COOKER

Slow cookers are very energy-efficient; most operate between 75 and 300 watts, the same as a typical table lamp. The thick stoneware crock retains heat for a long time, too, so you can unplug the machine—or even remove the crock from the base—when the food is ready, and the food will stay warm for an hour or longer.

BARBECUED VENISON RIBS

4 servings
Prep: 30 minutes
Cooking: 10 to 11½ hours on low, or 5 to 5½ hours on high
Slow cooker: Standard or Large

4 pounds (1.8 kg) meaty venison ribs*, cut apart
1 can (6 ounces/170 g) tomato paste
½ cup (120 ml) applesauce
½ cup (120 ml) honey
2 tablespoons (30 ml) cider vinegar
1 tablespoon (15 ml) Worcestershire sauce
1 teaspoon (5 ml) chili powder blend
½ teaspoon (2.5 ml) Tabasco sauce
½ teaspoon (2.5 ml) liquid smoke, optional
Half of a medium onion, cut into several chunks
2 cloves garlic

Heat a large pot of water to boiling. Add ribs; return to boiling, then reduce heat and simmer for 5 minutes. Remove ribs with tongs, and pat dry with paper towels. Place ribs in slow cooker.

In blender, combine remaining ingredients. Blend until sauce is chunky-smooth. Pour over ribs in slow cooker, turning to coat. Cover and cook until ribs are tender, 10 to 11½ hours on low or 5 to 5½ hours on high. Serve ribs with sauce.

*For meaty venison ribs, leave a portion of the loin, or an extra outer layer of meat, attached to ribs when butchering.

THICKENING COOKING JUICES

If you've prepared a stew or other dish that includes a fair amount of liquid, you may want to thicken the cooking liquid at the end of the cooking time. There are several ways to do this. Start by blending a tablespoon (15 ml) or so of cornstarch into just enough water to make a slurry (not a paste; that's too hard to incorporate); if you prefer flour, double the amounts. Add a bit of the liquid from the cooker and stir that in; then stir the mixture into the cooker or saucepan, depending on the method you're using, below.

• If your slow cooker gets hot enough to boil liquid, you can thicken the liquid right in the slow cooker. Add the cornstarch or flour mixture to the cooker, re-cover and increase the heat to high (if necessary). Generally, the liquid will thicken in 15 to 30 minutes. Note that older slow cookers may not get hot enough to boil liquid.

• The second method is to thicken the liquid on the stovetop. Use a slotted spoon to transfer the larger pieces of meat and vegetables to a serving dish; cover and keep warm. Pour the remaining mixture carefully into a saucepan. Whisk the cornstarch or flour mixture into the liquid in the saucepan, then heat over medium-high heat, stirring frequently, until the mixture thickens. This usually takes 10 minutes or less.

As an option, you could stir a tablespoon or two (15 to 30 ml) of quick-cooking tapioca into the liquid in the slow cooker; re-cover and cook until the mixture thickens, usually 5 to 10 minutes. Tapioca has a more noticeable texture than either cornstarch or flour.

RABBIT AND HOMINY STEW

4 to 6 servings
Prep: 15 minutes (plus additional for boning rabbit if not already boned; see page 84 sidebar)
Cooking: 7 to 8 hours on low, or 3 to 4 hours on high
Slow cooker: Standard

Hominy, which is also called *posole* or *pozole*, is dried corn kernels that have been soaked in a special mixture that swells the kernels; the hull is removed after soaking. Hominy has a pleasantly chewy texture and a rich corn taste. Look for hominy with the canned vegetables.

1 to 1¼ pounds (454 to 570 g) boneless rabbit meat, cut into bite-sized pieces
2 cans (15½ ounces/439 g) hominy (preferably one yellow and one white),
    drained and rinsed
1 cup (235 ml) chicken broth
1 can (4½ ounces/127 g) chopped green chiles
1 red bell pepper, diced
1 large onion, diced
3 cloves garlic, minced
2 tablespoons (30 ml) cornmeal
1 tablespoon (15 ml) ground cumin
1 tablespoon (15 ml) dried oregano leaves
1 teaspoon (5 ml) paprika
½ teaspoon (2.5 ml) salt
¼ to ½ teaspoon (1.25 to 2.5 ml) chipotle powder, optional (see sidebar on page 30)
¼ cup (60 ml) chopped fresh cilantro, optional (but highly recommended)
3 green onions, minced (white and green parts)
Accompaniments: Warmed flour tortillas, diced avocado, lime wedges, shredded cheese

In slow cooker, combine all ingredients except cilantro, green onions and accompaniments; stir well. Cover and cook until rabbit is tender, 7 to 8 hours on low, or 3 to 4 hours on high. About 5 minutes before serving, stir in cilantro and green onions. Serve with accompaniments of your choice.

SWEET AND SOUR RABBIT

5 or 6 servings
Prep: 15 minutes
Cooking: 7 to 8 hours on low (can cook up to 9 hours)
Slow cooker: Standard

For a pretty dish, use a mix of red and green bell pepper pieces.

12 to 15 baby-sized carrots, each cut into 2 shorter pieces
1 large green or red bell pepper, cut into large dice
1 small onion, cut into 8 vertical wedges
1½ pounds (675 g) boneless rabbit meat, cut into small bite-sized pieces
1 can (8 ounces/227 g) pineapple chunks packed in juice, undrained
⅓ cup (80 ml) seasoned rice vinegar*
¼ cup (60 ml/55 g) packed brown sugar
2 tablespoons (30 ml) quick-cooking tapioca
2 tablespoons (30 ml) soy sauce
1 tablespoon (15 ml) chopped fresh gingerroot
½ teaspoon (2.5 ml) hot red pepper flakes, optional
1 clove garlic, pressed or finely minced
Hot cooked rice

In slow cooker, combine carrots, bell pepper and onion, stirring to mix. Arrange rabbit meat on top of vegetables. In mixing bowl, combine remaining ingredients except rice, stirring to blend. Pour over rabbit and vegetables. Cover and cook on low for 7 to 8 hours; the rabbit can cook up to 9 hours. Serve over hot cooked rice.

*If you don't have any seasoned rice vinegar, substitute ¼ cup (60 ml) cider vinegar mixed with 2 teaspoons (10 ml) white sugar and 1 tablespoon (15 ml) water.

 REMOVING BONES FROM RABBITS

The backstrap (loin) is the largest piece of solid meat on a rabbit, and is easy to bone; simply cut the thick strip of meat away from the backbone and remove any fat. The legs are trickier to bone, and take a bit of time; use a sharp-tipped paring knife and cut as close to the bone as possible. To make it easier to prepare a recipe such as Sweet and Sour Rabbit or Rabbit and Hominy Stew, separate rabbit pieces by type when you're packing several for the freezer. Put boneless backstrap pieces in one package, and bone-in legs in another. This way, you can quickly and easily choose boneless rabbit meat when that's what you need; save the bone-in legs for recipes where the bones don't need to be removed.

RABBIT WITH SWEET RED PEPPERS

6 servings
Prep: 15 minutes
Cooking: 7 to 8 hours on low (can cook up to 9 hours)
Slow cooker: Standard

2 wild rabbits, cut into serving pieces
½ teaspoon (2.5 ml) salt
1 small onion, diced
2 tablespoons (30 ml) olive oil
½ cup (120 ml) chicken broth
2 cloves garlic, thinly sliced
2 tablespoons (30 ml/15 g) all-purpose flour
2 tablespoons (30 ml) tomato paste
1 tablespoon (15 ml/10 g) drained capers
1 teaspoon (5 ml) paprika

¼ teaspoon (1.25 ml) white pepper
A pinch of saffron (crumble if using
   saffron threads)
1 can (14½ ounces/411 g)
   diced tomatoes, drained
1 jar (12 ounces/340 g) roasted
   red bell peppers, drained and
   cut into ½-inch (1.25 cm) strips
Hot cooked rice or noodles

Pat rabbit pieces dry with paper towels. Sprinkle with salt; set aside for 5 minutes. Meanwhile, scatter onion inside slow cooker. In large skillet, heat oil over medium heat until shimmering. Add rabbit, and cook until golden on all sides. Transfer rabbit to slow cooker. In measuring cup, combine broth, garlic, flour, tomato paste, capers, paprika, white pepper and saffron; stir to blend. Pour over rabbit in slow cooker. Scatter drained tomatoes and roasted peppers over rabbit. Cover and cook on low for 7 to 8 hours, or until rabbit is very tender; rabbit can cook up to 9 hours. Serve with rice.

VARIATION: UPLAND GAMEBIRDS WITH SWEET RED PEPPERS
Substitute 3 partridge, 2 pheasants, or the breast portions from 3 pheasants, for the rabbits in the above recipe. Cut the birds into standard cooking pieces: breast halves with or without wings, legs and thighs (or leg/thigh combinations). Proceed as directed; cook on low for 7 hours (this can cook up to 8 hours on low).

CREAMY MUSHROOM SQUIRREL BAKE

4 or 5 servings
Prep: 15 minutes, plus a bit of additional prep shortly before serving
Cooking: 7 to 8 hours on low, plus 15 to 30 minutes on high just before serving
Slow cooker: Standard

Serve this with rice or with curly, wide noodles to catch all the sauce.

2 squirrels, cut into serving pieces
Salt and pepper
4 slices bacon, diced
8 ounces (225 g) fresh mushrooms, sliced
1 medium onion, diced
1 can (14½ ounces/411 g) beef broth
1 tablespoon (15 ml) lemon juice
2 teaspoons (10 ml) Dijon mustard
1 cup (235 ml/227 g) sour cream
3 tablespoons (45 ml) all-purpose flour
½ teaspoon (2.5 ml) dried marjoram or thyme leaves
Paprika

Pat squirrel pieces dry. Sprinkle generously with salt and pepper; arrange in slow cooker. In large skillet, cook bacon over medium heat until just crisp, stirring frequently. Add mushrooms and onion. Increase heat to medium-high and cook, stirring frequently, for about 5 minutes. Scrape mushroom mixture into slow cooker. Add broth, lemon juice and mustard to skillet, stirring to blend. Cook over high heat for a minute or so, then pour broth into slow cooker. Cover and cook on low until squirrel is tender, 7 to 8 hours.

Shortly before you're ready to serve, spoon out about ⅓ cup (80 ml) of the liquid from the slow cooker into a bowl; increase slow cooker to high. Add sour cream, flour and herbs to bowl with liquid, stirring to blend well. Add sour cream mixture to slow cooker, stirring to combine. Re-cover and cook until sauce thickens somewhat, 15 to 30 minutes. Sprinkle with paprika before serving.

 HOW FULL SHOULD THE SLOW COOKER BE?

Slow cookers work best when they are between half and two-thirds full. If you use less than this, the food may scorch or get overcooked; if the slow cooker is over-full, the food may boil over, or it may take a lot longer to get done. If you have a Personal or Small slow cooker, try cutting recipe ingredients in half; in most cases, this works fine. Cooking time may need to be reduced slightly.

CLASSIC BRUNSWICK STEW

6 to 8 servings
Prep: 15 minutes for first step; 15 minutes for second step
Cooking: 8 to 10 hours on low for first step; 6 hours on low or 3 hours on high for second step
   (can cook as long as 8 hours on low for second step)
Slow cooker: Standard

This is a two-step recipe. First, squirrel is stewed until it's tender. The meat is removed from the bone; then, the boned meat is combined with hearty vegetables and broth to make a rich stew. You can do the first step one day, then refrigerate the broth and meat for a day or two, until you're ready for the final cooking. Serve this with hot buttered biscuits.

STEP 1:

3 squirrels
1 quart (1 liter) chicken broth
2 ribs celery, broken into 3 pieces each
1 medium onion, cut into quarters
1 bay leaf

STEP 2:

1 can (14½ ounces/411 g) whole tomatoes, undrained
1 can (10¾ ounces/305 g) condensed cream of celery soup
1 cup (235 ml) hot water
2 medium russet potatoes, peeled and diced
1 medium onion, diced
1 package (9 ounces/255 g) frozen lima beans, thawed
1 cup (235 ml/165 g) frozen whole-kernel corn, thawed
1 tablespoon (15 ml) packed brown sugar
1 tablespoon (15 ml) Worcestershire sauce
¼ teaspoon (1.25 ml) freshly ground black pepper
4 or 5 dashes Tabasco sauce

FOR STEP 1: In slow cooker, combine all ingredients listed in step 1. Cover and cook on low until squirrel is tender, 8 to 10 hours. Remove squirrel from broth and set aside to cool. Strain and reserve broth; discard solids. When squirrel is cool enough to handle, remove meat from bones; discard bones. At this point, the broth and squirrel meat can be refrigerated, covered, overnight or as long as 2 days.

FOR STEP 2: In slow cooker, combine cooked squirrel meat, reserved broth, and all ingredients listed in step 2. Cover and cook on low for 6 hours, or on high for 3 hours; stew can cook as long as 8 hours on low.

COUNTRY-STYLE SQUIRREL STEW

5 or 6 servings
Prep: 15 minutes
Cooking: 7 to 8 hours on low
Slow cooker: Standard or Large

Serve this down-home, simple stew with cornbread and coleslaw.

2 large onions, cut into quarters and sliced
2 squirrels, cut into serving pieces
1 teaspoon (5 ml) Worcestershire sauce
½ teaspoon (2.5 ml) salt
½ teaspoon (2.5 ml) pepper
1 green or red bell pepper, cut into 1-inch (2.5 cm) cubes
1 pound (454 g) baby-sized carrots
1 pound (454 g) small red or Yukon gold potatoes
1 cup (235 ml) chicken broth
1 tablespoon (15 ml) all-purpose flour

Spread onions in bottom of slow cooker. Arrange squirrel pieces on top, tucking together snugly in the center of the slow cooker. Sprinkle squirrel with Worcestershire sauce, salt and pepper. Scatter bell pepper pieces over squirrel. Tuck carrots and potatoes around the outside edges of the slow cooker. In mixing bowl, blend together broth and flour; pour into slow cooker. Cover and cook on low until squirrel is tender, 7 to 8 hours.

 COOKING TIME AND AGE OF SMALL GAME

Squirrels and rabbits are relatively tender when they're young, but older specimens tend to be tough, requiring longer cooking. Before skinning the game, check for clues as to the relative age. Young squirrels have a pointed, tapering tail, while older squirrels tend to have straight tails with blunt ends. A young rabbit has soft, flexible ears and a small cleft in the upper lip; ears on an older rabbit are stiff, and the cleft tends to be deeper. It's helpful to mark packages of small game as you prepare it for the freezer, noting whether the game is young or mature. If you've thawed some frozen small game that isn't marked, look at the color of the meat. Older animals generally have darker meat than younger animals.

When you're cooking small game in the slow cooker, check it for tenderness at the lower time listed by poking it with a fork. If it doesn't yield easily, re-cover quickly and continue cooking until it is tender. Boneless pieces will cook more quickly than bone-in pieces. I find that the low setting is preferable for bone-in pieces; the high-heat setting seems to cause the meat to shrink and toughen.

SQUIRREL OR RABBIT WITH MUSTARD

5 or 6 servings
Prep: 15 minutes
Cooking: 7 to 8 hours on low
Slow cooker: Standard or Large

Mustard and blue cheese complement each other very well in this easy dish. Serve with rice, salad and a vegetable.

2 wild rabbits or 3 squirrels, cut into serving pieces
Salt and pepper
2 tablespoons (30 ml) olive oil or vegetable oil
1 medium onion, diced
1 cup (235 ml) chicken broth
½ cup (120 ml) dry white wine
¼ cup (60 ml) Dijon mustard
2 tablespoons (30 ml) all-purpose flour
1 teaspoon (5 ml) dried thyme leaves
¼ cup (60 ml/60 g) blue cheese crumbles
1 tablespoon (15 ml) chopped fresh parsley

Pat rabbit or squirrel pieces dry; season generously with salt and pepper. In Dutch oven, heat oil over medium heat until shimmering. Add game pieces and brown lightly on all sides. Use tongs to transfer game pieces to slow cooker. Add onion to Dutch oven; sauté until just tender-crisp, about 5 minutes. In small bowl, blend together broth, wine, mustard and flour until smooth. Add broth mixture and thyme to Dutch oven. Cook over medium heat, stirring frequently, until sauce bubbles and thickens a bit. Pour sauce over game pieces in slow cooker. Cover and cook on low until game pieces are tender, 7 to 8 hours. A few minutes before serving, sprinkle blue cheese into slow cooker; re-cover and let stand until cheese melts. Sprinkle with parsley before serving.

HONEY-MUSTARD PHEASANT

4 servings
Prep: 15 minutes
Cooking: 7 hours on low
Slow cooker: Standard

The various flavors—honey, mustard, orange and curry—combine to make a delicious, somewhat sweet sauce. The insides of the orange slices get very soft, and taste good; the peel, while it can be eaten, is a bit strong for most people, so you may choose to remove the orange slices before serving. For a milder orange flavor, peel the orange before slicing; that way, you don't have to worry about removing the orange slices.

1 orange, well washed, sliced (peel before slicing if you like; see note above)
1 medium onion, sliced
Bone-in breast halves from 2 pheasants, skin removed (4 pieces total)
Salt
¹⁄₃ cup (80 ml) honey
¹⁄₃ cup (80 ml) prepared mustard
2 tablespoons (30 ml) orange juice
¹⁄₂ teaspoon (2.5 ml) curry powder blend
2 tablespoons (30 g/30 ml) butter, cut up

Arrange orange slices evenly in bottom of slow cooker. Top with onion. Place pheasant breast halves over onion; sprinkle with salt to taste. In small bowl, stir together honey, mustard, orange juice and curry powder until smooth. Pour honey mixture over pheasant; dot with butter. Cover and cook on low for 7 hours.

---

 3 SLOW-COOKER SAFETY TIPS

Slow cookers are safe appliances—when used correctly. Here are 3 safety tips to keep in mind; you should also review the Use and Care information that may have come with your slow cooker when you purchased it.

• *Before use, check that the handles on the base are intact and securely attached; they have been known to come off. If they seem loose, contact the manufacturer for instructions; they may replace the unit for you.*

• *If the power cord becomes damaged, don't use the appliance. Return it to the manufacturer for service, or simply replace the unit.*

• *The outside of the slow cooker gets hot. Always set the appliance on a heat-proof surface, away from curtains, towels, papers and other easily flammable materials.*

PHEASANT AND DUMPLINGS

4 or 5 servings
Prep: 15 minutes, plus 15 minutes shortly before serving
Cooking: 7 hours on low (or 3 1/2 hours on high), followed by 45 minutes on high
Slow cooker: Standard

You can substitute partridge, turkey or grouse for the pheasant in this classic comfort-food recipe. Plan this for a day when you'll have time for a little last-minute prep and final cooking.

3 carrots, sliced
1 rib celery, diced
1 small onion, diced
1 teaspoon (5 ml) dried herb blend
1 bay leaf
2 pheasants, cut up and skin removed, or equivalent in pieces (about 3 pounds/1.4 kg)
1 can (10 3/4 ounces/305 g) condensed reduced-fat cream of chicken soup
3 cups (690 ml) chicken broth
1 tube (10 to 12 ounces/289 to 340 g) refrigerated buttermilk biscuits*

Combine carrots, celery, onion, herbs and bay leaf in slow cooker; stir to mix up. Arrange cut-up pheasant on top, with the legs and thighs on the bottom and the breast portions on top. In mixing bowl, stir together soup and broth. Pour soup mixture over pheasant. Cover and cook on low for 7 hours, or on high for 3 1/2 hours. With slotted spoon, transfer pheasant pieces to cutting board and set aside to cool slightly. Use slotted spoon to pick through mixture in slow cooker to remove any bones. Remove and discard bay leaf.

Remove pheasant meat from bones; discard bones and any tendons. Tear pheasant into large bite-sized pieces; return to slow cooker and stir gently. Separate biscuits, and cut each in half if large. Arrange biscuit pieces over pheasant mixture. Re-cover slow cooker; increase heat to high if necessary. Cook for 45 to 50 minutes longer, or until dumplings are cooked through; they will no longer look wet on the top, and will feel springy when pressed with a fingertip. Serve in soup plates; caution diners to watch for stray bones that may have escaped your notice.

*Substitute dumplings made from buttermilk baking mix if you prefer. Follow package directions for dumplings on the box of baking mix. Drop in heaping tablespoons onto pheasant mix; cook as directed above.

PHEASANT BRAISED WITH WHOLE GARLIC

4 servings
Prep: 15 minutes
Cooking: 7 hours on low (can cook up to 8 hours)
Slow cooker: Small or Standard

This dish contains a whole head of garlic, but don't worry—the garlic becomes mellow and sweet when cooked in this fashion.

Boneless, skinless breast halves from 2 pheasants (4 pieces total)
Seasoned salt
All-purpose flour for dredging
2 tablespoons (30 g/30 ml) butter
1 cup (235 ml) chicken broth
½ teaspoon (2.5 ml) dried marjoram or oregano leaves
¼ teaspoon (1.25 ml) crumbled dried rosemary leaves
¼ teaspoon (1.25 ml) sugar
¼ teaspoon (1.25 ml) salt
A pinch of ground saffron or ground turmeric
1 medium onion
1 small head garlic, loose outer skin removed
1 bay leaf

Pat pheasant dry with paper towels. Season generously with seasoned salt. Dredge in flour, shaking off excess. Heat butter over medium heat in medium skillet. Add pheasant; brown lightly on both sides.

While pheasant is browning, add chicken broth, marjoram, rosemary, sugar, salt and saffron to slow cooker; stir to mix. Cut onion into quarters from top to bottom, then slice each quarter ⅛ inch (3 mm) thick. Add onions, whole garlic head and bay leaf to slow cooker. When pheasant has browned, transfer to slow cooker, arranging on top of onions. Cover and cook on low for 7 hours; pheasant can cook for as long as 8 hours. Remove garlic and allow to cool enough to handle, then squeeze cloves back into dish, discarding skins. Thicken juices if you like (see page 82) and serve with pheasant.

 HERBS AND SEASONINGS

Some seasonings, such as bay leaves, cinnamon sticks, whole peppercorns or whole dried peppers, need long simmering to bring out their flavor; these work well in slow-cooked dishes. (You may want to tie them in a small square of cheesecloth, so you can easily remove them from the finished dish.) Dried leafy herbs may lose their punch during long cooking; you may wish to taste the sauce just prior to serving, and punch it up with a bit more of whatever herb was used. Chopped fresh herbs should be added at the end of cooking time; a few minutes' standing time is all it takes to draw out the flavor.

STUFFED POACHED UPLAND ROLL

5 or 6 main-dish servings (hot), or 8 to 10 luncheon servings (cold)
Prep: 30 minutes
Cooking: 4 hours on low, plus 30 minutes stovetop cooking for optional sauce
Slow cooker: Standard or Large, oval

Serve this warm as a dinner entrée, or refrigerate and serve cold on a luncheon salad plate. This recipe works well with shot-up birds that might not look so good when prepared whole; be sure to pick out all shot and any bone fragments.

2 cups (475 ml/140 g) fresh spinach leaves, tightly packed
2 eggs
1 tablespoon (15 ml) cornstarch
1 tablespoon (15 ml) olive oil or vegetable oil
1 teaspoon (5 ml) dried oregano leaves
½ teaspoon (2.5 ml) salt
½ cup (120 ml) seasoned bread crumbs
1 jar (4 ounces/113 g) sliced pimientos, drained
1 tablespoon (15 ml) drained capers, optional
1¼ pounds (570 g) boneless, skinless turkey, pheasant or other upland gamebird meat
1 small onion

1 quart (1 liter) chicken broth
1 cup (235 ml) white wine
1 bay leaf
1 dried hot red pepper, optional
8 whole black peppercorns
1 tablespoon plus 1½ teaspoons (22.5 ml) cornstarch dissolved in ¼ cup (60 ml) cold water, optional (for sauce)
You'll also need: Large piece of cheesecloth (36 x 36 inches/ 91 x 91 cm), several pieces of heavy kitchen string

Blanch spinach in saucepan of boiling water for 30 seconds; drain and refresh immediately with cold water. Let drain while you prepare other ingredients. In large mixing bowl, beat together eggs, cornstarch, oil, oregano and salt with a fork until smooth. Stir in bread crumbs, pimientos and capers; set aside.

Cut meat into 1½-inch (4 cm) cubes; transfer to food processor fitted with metal chopping blade. Pulse on-and-off until chopped to medium consistency (a bit coarser than hamburger). Transfer meat to bowl with egg mixture. Cut onion into quarters, then chop medium-fine in food processor; add to meat. Mix gently but thoroughly with your hands.

Open up and re-fold cheesecloth so you have a double layer that is 18 x 36 inches (46 x 91 cm), then place on worksurface with an 18-inch (46 cm) edge nearest you. Place meat mixture on cheesecloth and pat into a 9 x 7-inch (23 x 18 cm) rectangle, about an inch (2.5 cm) from the edge of the cheesecloth closest to you. Squeeze spinach dry, then arrange in a line along the center of the meat, parallel with the 9-inch (23 cm) edge. Use the cheesecloth to lift the meat up, shaping it into a roll (don't roll the cheesecloth up inside the roll). Twist ends together and tie with kitchen string. Place roll into slow cooker. Add broth, wine, bay leaf, hot pepper and peppercorns. If liquid doesn't cover roll, add water as necessary. Cover and cook on low for 4 hours. Carefully transfer roll to large plate (I use tongs and a spatula); remove cheesecloth gently while roll is still hot. Cover and keep warm while you make sauce; or cover and refrigerate until cold before slicing (the sauce is not used if serving the roll cold).

TO MAKE SAUCE:

Strain cooking liquid into medium saucepan. Cook on stovetop over medium-high heat until reduced to 1½ cups (350 ml). Whisking constantly, add cornstarch mixture; cook, stirring frequently, until sauce thickens and bubbles. Serve sauce with sliced roll.

SMALL BIRDS FOR TWO

2 servings
Prep: 15 minutes, plus a bit of additional prep shortly before serving
Cooking: 6 hours on low, followed by 15 to 20 minutes on high
Slow cooker: Personal

Here's an elegant meal for two, prepared in a small slow cooker. I use my 1.5-quart (1.5 liter) model, but the 2.5-quart (2.25 liter) model also works. Serve with rice, to soak up all the savory mushroom cream sauce.

1 tablespoon (15 g/15 ml)
   butter or margarine
4 to 6 ounces (115 to 170 g)
   fresh mushrooms
   (preferably a blend), sliced
3 tablespoons (45 ml) dry sherry
2 tablespoons (30 ml) water
4 whole quail, woodcock or doves*,
   skin removed

Salt-based seasoning blend (such as
   Montreal seasoning), or plain salt
   and pepper
1/3 cup (80 ml) sour cream
1 tablespoon (15 ml) cornstarch
1 tablespoon (15 ml) grated
   Parmesan cheese

In large skillet, melt butter over medium-high heat. Add mushrooms, spreading evenly. Cook without stirring until mushrooms begin to brown, 3 to 5 minutes. Stir and continue cooking for 3 to 5 minutes longer, until the second side is nicely browned. Scrape mushrooms into slow cooker. Add sherry and water to slow cooker.

Rinse birds and pat dry with paper towels. Sprinkle generously with your favorite salt-based seasoning blend. Tuck birds, breast-sides down, into slow cooker. Cover and cook on low for 6 hours, or until birds are tender (the flesh on the drumsticks should pull away from the bottoms of the bone). Increase slow cooker to high. Use tongs and a large slotted spoon to gently transfer the birds to a serving dish; cover to keep warm and set aside.

In measuring cup or small bowl, combine sour cream, cornstarch, and about 2 tablespoons (30 ml) of the cooking juices, stirring to blend. Stir sour cream mixture into slow cooker. Re-cover and cook on high for 15 to 20 minutes, or until juices have thickened somewhat. Pour mixture over birds in serving dish; sprinkle with Parmesan cheese. See sidebar on page 95 for a note about small bones.

You could also substitute 4 to 6 whole, bone-in breast portions for the whole birds, if that is what you have. Many hunters keep only the breast portions of small gamebirds, and that's a shame, for the legs and thighs of these small birds are delicious and should be savored. Ethics—and good cooking—dictate that the entire bird should be used.

DOVE AND CORNBREAD CASSEROLE

4 to 6 servings
Prep: 15 minutes
Cooking: 4 1/2 hours on low (can cook up to 5 hours)
Slow cooker: Standard

Dove breasts are surrounded by a rich, moist cornbread stuffing mix in this adaptation of a classic Southern recipe. If you like, substitute 6 boneless, skinless Hungarian partridge breasts or 6 whole dove or quail, split in half, for the dove breasts. This recipe makes a lot of stuffing; if you don't eat all of it with the birds, it can be reheated for another meal.

1/4 cup (55 g/half of a stick) butter
2 ribs celery, thinly sliced
Half of a medium onion, diced
1 bag (16 ounces/454 g) finely textured cornbread stuffing mix
2 cups (475 ml) beef broth or chicken broth
1 teaspoon (5 ml) dried herb blend of your choice
1/2 teaspoon (2.5 ml) seasoned salt or plain salt
8 to 10 bone-in dove breasts, or substitute (see note above)

In Dutch oven or very large skillet, melt butter over medium heat. Brush a generous amount of butter inside slow cooker; set slow cooker aside. Add celery and onion to Dutch oven with remaining butter; sauté until tender-crisp, about 5 minutes. Add stuffing, broth, herbs and salt to Dutch oven; stir until stuffing is evenly moistened. Place half of the stuffing mixture into slow cooker. Arrange dove breasts over stuffing, pushing them down slightly into the stuffing. Cover with remaining stuffing mixture. Cover and cook on low for 4 1/2 hours; casserole can cook up to 5 hours.

 SMALL BIRDS AND THE SLOW COOKER

The slow cooker tenderizes poultry so much that it may begin to fall apart when you serve it. Bones from larger birds, such as turkey and pheasant, are easy to pick out or nibble around, but those of smaller birds such as quail, dove and woodcock are harder to deal with. One way to avoid some of the bones is to cut out and discard the backbone before cooking, using kitchen shears.

When eating small gamebirds that have been tenderized in the slow cooker, watch for the bones, much as you do when eating fish; be sure to tell other diners as well. Don't be too shy to use your fingers to pick up and enjoy every morsel, as though you were eating a tiny fried chicken drumstick. Keep a pretty dish on the table for the discarded bones.

CURRIED PHEASANT OR TURKEY

5 or 6 servings
Prep: 15 minutes, plus a bit of additional prep shortly before serving
Cooking: 6 1/2 hours on low, or 3 hours on high (can cook up to 8 hours on low),
*   plus 15 minutes on high shortly before serving*
Slow cooker: Standard or Large

Spicy-sweet, with an exotic flavor, this curry is a perfect warmer for winter weather. Be sure to buy unsweetened coconut milk (found with the Asian staples at a supermarket), not the thicker, sweetened coconut cream that is used for tropical drinks.

1 pound (454 g) boneless, skinless pheasant or turkey meat, cut into bite-sized pieces
1 pound (454 g) orange-fleshed sweet potatoes* (about 2 medium), peeled and cut into
**   1-inch (2.5 cm) chunks**
1 green bell pepper, cut into 1-inch (2.5 cm) chunks
1 red bell pepper, cut into 1-inch (2.5 cm) chunks
1 medium Vidalia or other sweet onion, cut into 3/4-inch (2 cm) chunks
1 can (14 1/2 ounces/411 g) diced tomatoes, undrained
3 tablespoons (45 ml) peanut butter, crunchy or smooth
1 tablespoon (15 ml) curry powder blend
1 tablespoon (15 ml) minced fresh gingerroot
2 teaspoons (10 ml) minced garlic
1/2 teaspoon (2.5 ml) ground cumin
1/4 to 1/2 teaspoon (1.25 to 2.5 ml) hot red pepper flakes
3/4 cup (180 ml) unsweetened coconut milk
2 tablespoons (30 ml) all-purpose flour
For serving: Hot cooked rice, chopped peanuts

In slow cooker, combine pheasant, sweet potatoes, bell peppers and onion; stir to mix. In small bowl, combine tomatoes with their juices, peanut butter, curry powder, gingerroot, garlic, cumin and hot pepper flakes; stir to blend peanut butter. Pour mixture into slow cooker. Cover and cook on low for 6 1/2 hours, or on high for 3 hours; the curry can cook up to 8 hours on low. When you're almost ready to serve, increase slow cooker to high if necessary. In small bowl, combine coconut milk and flour, stirring to blend. Add to slow cooker, stirring well. Re-cover and cook on high until sauce thickens somewhat, about 15 minutes. Serve curry over hot cooked rice; sprinkle with peanuts.

*Orange-fleshed sweet potatoes are often called yams; see the sidebar on page 119 for more information.

BIRDS AND BISCUITS

4 servings
Prep: 15 minutes, plus a bit of additional prep shortly before serving
Cooking: 6½ hours on low (can cook up to 8 hours), plus 15 to 30 minutes on high
Slow cooker: Standard

This down-home dish practically makes itself. While the gravy is thickening at the end, all you need to do is whip up a batch of biscuits (use refrigerated buttermilk biscuits for extra-quick prep) and toss a salad.

1 pound (454 g) boneless, skinless upland gamebird meat, cut into
   ½-inch (1.25 cm) pieces
12 frozen pearl onions, thawed, cut in half
3 carrots, diced
1 jar (2 ounces/57 g) diced pimientos, drained
½ cup (120 ml) chicken broth
½ teaspoon (2.5 ml) seasoned salt
¾ cup (180 ml) evaporated fat-free milk
1 tablespoon (15 ml) all-purpose flour
1 envelope (generally about 1 ounce/28 g, depending on brand) roasted chicken
   gravy mix
1 cup (235 ml/200 g) frozen green peas, thawed (do not substitute canned peas)
Hot biscuits prepared from refrigerated biscuits, boxed buttermilk baking mix or
   homemade

In slow cooker, combine gamebird meat, onions, carrots, pimientos, broth and salt; stir to mix. Cover and cook on low for 6½ hours; this can cook as long as 8 hours.

Thirty minutes before serving, combine evaporated milk, flour and gravy mix in mixing bowl; whisk until smooth. Add milk mixture and peas to slow cooker, stirring well. Re-cover; increase heat to high and cook until gravy has thickened and peas are cooked, 15 to 30 minutes. While gravy is thickening, prepare biscuits. Spoon bird mixture over split biscuits.

MILK, CREAM AND CHEESE

Dairy foods break down and curdle during long, slow cooking. Creamy condensed soups, such as cream of mushroom, have stabilizers added, so these can be used to add creaminess to dishes. Evaporated milk is more stable than fresh milk and can handle up to an hour of cooking time; it's generally added near the end of cooking time. Sour cream, fresh cream and most cheeses are best if stirred into the dish just before serving. For best results, don't allow the mixture to boil after adding these dairy ingredients.

PHEASANT-STUFFED MANICOTTI

4 servings
Prep: 30 minutes, plus a bit of additional prep shortly before serving
Cooking: 4 hours on low, plus 5 minutes stovetop cooking shortly before serving
Slow cooker: Standard or Large

Manicotti is a large tubular pasta, generally about 4½ x 1½ inches (11 x 4 cm). It can be found with the other dried pastas at well-stocked grocery stores. You'll also find ready-to-serve Alfredo sauce in the same aisle. Feel free to substitute any jarred Alfredo-style sauce for the mushroom-enriched sauce used here.

**6 ounces (170 g) boneless,
  skinless pheasant meat***
**¼ pound (113 g) bulk pork breakfast
  sausage, such as Jimmy Dean's (mild)**
**1 jar (16 ounces/454 g) Alfredo-style sauce
  with mushrooms, divided**
¾ cup (180 ml) water
1 egg

⅓ cup (80 ml) reduced-fat ricotta cheese
**½ cup (120 ml/30 g) fresh bread crumbs
  (see below)**
**⅓ cup (42 g/80 ml) shredded Parmesan or
  Romano cheese**
**1 package (8 ounces/226 g) manicotti
  shells, uncooked**

Add pheasant to food processor fitted with metal blade; pulse on-and-off until chopped to hamburger consistency (be careful not to over-process; it chops quite quickly). Spray large skillet with nonstick spray. Add pheasant and sausage; cook over medium heat, stirring frequently to break up, until meat is no longer pink. Set aside to cool slightly.

In large measuring cup (or small mixing bowl), stir together 1 cup (235 ml) of the Alfredo sauce and the water; refrigerate remaining sauce. In medium mixing bowl, beat together egg and ricotta with a fork. Add bread crumbs, Parmesan and cooled pheasant mixture; mix gently but thoroughly. Stuff mixture into uncooked manicotti shells. Arrange one-third of the stuffed shells in slow cooker; spray lightly with cooking spray. Pour one-third of the sauce mixture over the shells. Repeat with remaining shells and sauce, for a total of 3 layers. Cover and cook on low for 4 hours; if possible, baste shells with sauce midway through cooking (use a bulb baster to collect sauce from the sides of the dish, then squeeze it over the top layer of shells; work quickly to avoid losing heat).

Just before serving, heat remaining sauce on the stovetop, then pour over cooked shells.

*Substitute boneless rabbit meat, or the meat from any upland gamebird, for the pheasant.

 HOW TO MAKE FRESH BREAD CRUMBS

Fresh bread crumbs are much moister and fluffier than dry bread crumbs; they help provide a more uniform tex-
ture in stuffings and meat loaf without absorbing too much of the moisture from the rest of the ingredients. To
prepare fresh bread crumbs, use sliced day-old French or Italian bread. Cut bread into 1-inch (2.5 cm) pieces.
Start empty blender (or food processor fitted with metal chopping blade). Drop bread cubes into running machine
through the hole in the top of the blender lid (or through processor feed tube); chop to medium-fine consistency.
Be sure to keep lid on as much as possible; the crumbs tend to jump out of the machine during chopping. An aver-
age-sized slice of bread (3 x 4 x ¾ inches/7.5 x 10 x 2 cm) will make about a cup (235 ml) of fresh bread crumbs.

Black Bean, Pumpkin and Gamebird Stew

4 or 5 servings
Prep: 15 minutes
Cooking: 6¼ hours on low (can cook up to 8 hours)
Slow cooker: Standard

Be sure to buy a cooking pumpkin for this Mexican-inspired stew—not a Jack o' Lantern! If you can't find a small pumpkin, substitute butternut or another hard squash. Dark meat, such as that from Hungarian partridge or sharptail grouse, is excellent in this stew, but you can use pheasant, turkey or any other upland gamebird.

1 large Vidalia or other sweet onion
1 pound (454 g) boneless, skinless upland gamebird meat, cut into bite-sized pieces
1 tablespoon (15 ml) cocoa powder (the kind used for baking)
2 teaspoons (10 ml) dried oregano leaves
1 teaspoon (5 ml) salt
½ teaspoon (2.5 ml) ground cinnamon
¼ teaspoon (1.25 ml) white pepper
3 cloves garlic, chopped
Small cooking pumpkin (a 1½-pound/680 g pumpkin is perfect)
1 can (15 ounces/425 g) black beans with cumin, undrained*
½ cup (120 ml) chicken broth or water
1 tablespoon (15 ml) quick-cooking tapioca
2 teaspoons (10 ml) red wine vinegar
Hot cooked couscous or rice

Cut onion into quarters from top to bottom, then slice each quarter ½ inch (1.25 cm) thick. Scatter onion in slow cooker. In mixing bowl, combine gamebird meat, cocoa powder, oregano, salt, cinnamon, pepper and garlic. Mix well with a wooden spoon, then distribute evenly over onion. Peel pumpkin and remove pulpy seed mass; weigh out 1 pound (454 g) of the cleaned pumpkin meat (refrigerate any remaining pumpkin for another use). Cut cleaned, weighed pumpkin into 1-inch (2.5 cm) cubes; distribute evenly over gamebird meat. In same mixing bowl, combine undrained beans, broth, tapioca and vinegar; stir well, then pour evenly over gamebird meat. Cover and cook on low for 6¼ hours; the stew can cook up to 8 hours, although the pumpkin will become quite soft. Serve over couscous or rice.

*If you can't find black beans with cumin, use regular black beans with ¼ teaspoon (1.25 ml) ground cumin added.

PARTRIDGE WITH APPLES AND BACON

2 or 3 servings (recipe is easily doubled)
Prep: 15 minutes
Cooking: 5½ to 6½ hours on low (can cook up to 7 hours on low)
Slow cooker: Small (double recipe for Regular or Large slow cooker)

Hungarian partridge has more flavor than pheasant, and works really well with the flavors of bacon and apple. Chukar partridge are a bit milder than Hungarian partridge, but are also delicious with this recipe. (I think that sharp-tailed grouse would also be good when prepared in this manner, but I've never had the chance to try it.)

1 large Macintosh or Braeburn apple
1 tablespoon (15 ml) orange juice
2 whole Hungarian or chukar partridge,
  skin removed

½ teaspoon (2.5 ml) dried
  marjoram leaves
Seasoned pepper or plain black pepper
4 slices bacon, cut in half crosswise

Peel, quarter and core apple. Slice ½ inch (1.25 cm) thick; distribute evenly in slow cooker. Sprinkle with orange juice. Cut partridge into halves (a game shears works well for this; simply cut along one side of the breastbone, then up the backbone). Rinse birds well, paying particular attention to the insides; pat dry with paper towels. Sprinkle with marjoram, and pepper to taste. One at a time, place a partridge half in the slow cooker, topping each half with 2 half slices of bacon. When all partridge have been placed in slow cooker, cover and cook until birds are very tender, 5½ to 6½ hours on low; the birds can cook as long as 7 hours. Serve birds with cooked apples and juices from slow cooker.

HOW MUCH MEAT WILL I GET FROM A...

Some recipes call for a specific amount, by weight, of boneless, skinless gamebird meat. Here's an approximate guide to what you can expect from the birds you're likely to use in this way. All yields are for the specific portion from one bird; for example, "Pheasant breast" means the two boneless, skinless breast halves from one pheasant.

SPECIES	OUNCES	GRAMS
Pheasant breast	8	225
Pheasant thighs	3½ to 4	100 to 115
Partridge or grouse breast	4	115
Dove breast	1	30
Mallard breast	6 to 8	170 to 225
Snow or other small goose breast	10 to 11	285 to 315

SPECIES	POUNDS	KILOGRAMS
Small Canada goose breast	12 to 16	340 to 454
Giant goose breast	1¼ to 3	0.6 to 1.4
Turkey breast	6½ to 7	3 to 3.2
Turkey thighs	1 to 1¼	0.5 to 0.6

PHEASANT LEGS CACCIATORE

4 servings
Prep: 30 minutes
Cooking: 7½ to 8½ hours on low
Slow cooker: Standard

When you're packaging pheasants for the freezer, cut them into parts, and package the drumsticks separately. The breasts and thighs can be cooked together in various dishes, but the drumsticks really need longer cooking to become tender. Here's a perfect recipe for them. Keep a pretty dish on the table for the discarded bones.

2 or 3 slices bacon, cut up
8 ounces (225 g) fresh mushrooms, sliced
2 large carrots, coarsely chopped
1 rib celery, coarsely chopped
1 medium onion, coarsely chopped
3 or 4 cloves garlic, minced
½ cup (120 ml) dry white wine
1 can (14½ ounces/411 g) diced tomatoes, undrained
2 tablespoons (30 ml) quick-cooking tapioca
1 tablespoon (15 ml) sugar
1 teaspoon (5 ml) salt
¼ teaspoon (1.25 ml) hot red pepper flakes
2 bay leaves
12 pheasant drumsticks*
1 teaspoon (5 ml) dried Italian herb blend
For serving: Hot cooked spaghetti, shredded Parmesan cheese

In large skillet, cook bacon over medium heat, stirring frequently, until just crisp. Add mushrooms, carrots, celery, onion and garlic; cook, stirring occasionally, for 5 minutes longer. Add wine; cook for about 5 minutes longer. Pour mixture into slow cooker. Add tomatoes with their juices, tapioca, sugar, salt and pepper flakes to slow cooker; stir well. Add bay leaves. Nestle drumsticks into sauce mixture. Cover and cook until drumsticks are very tender, 7½ to 8½ hours on low. Just before serving, remove and discard bay leaves; sprinkle herb blend into mixture and let stand for a few minutes. Serve over hot cooked spaghetti, passing Parmesan cheese separately. Alert diners that there may be a stray bone or tendon that has slipped from a drumstick into the sauce; these pieces are large enough to spot and don't cause a problem, but diners should be made aware of the possibility.

*You can also use a combination of drumsticks and thighs (cut them apart at the joint before cooking); the thigh meat gets tender a bit sooner, but it holds up fine.

DUCK OR GOOSE CASSOULET

5 or 6 servings
Prep: 30 minutes
Cooking: 6¼ hours on low
Equipment: Standard or Large

Serve this with a green salad, and crusty French bread to sop up the juices. If you have some smoked venison sausages, they would be a great choice for this dish.

4 ounces (113 g) thick-sliced bacon, cut into 1-inch (2.5 cm) pieces
8 ounces (225 g) smoked sausage links, cut into ½-inch (1.25 cm) pieces
1 can (14½ ounces/411 g) diced tomatoes, undrained
3 tablespoons (45 ml) tomato paste
½ teaspoon (2.5 ml) salt
1 onion, chopped
5 cloves garlic, thinly sliced
1 cup (235 ml) beef broth
1 pound (454 g) boneless, skinless duck (2 mallards) or goose meat,
  cut into 1-inch (2.5 cm) pieces
2 cans (15 to 19 ounces/425 to 538 g each) cannellini or Great Northern beans,
  drained and rinsed
1 bay leaf
½ teaspoon (2.5 ml) dried marjoram leaves
¼ teaspoon (1.25 ml) dried thyme leaves
¼ teaspoon (1.25 ml) crumbled dried rosemary leaves

In large skillet, cook bacon and sausage over medium heat, stirring frequently, until bacon is just crisp. While bacon is cooking, combine tomatoes with their juices, tomato paste and salt in slow cooker; stir to blend. When bacon is done, use slotted spoon to transfer bacon and sausage to slow cooker. Drain and discard most of the drippings from skillet. Add onion and garlic to skillet; sauté for about 5 minutes. Transfer onion mixture to slow cooker. Add broth to skillet, stirring to loosen any browned bits. Cook over medium-high heat for about 3 minutes, then pour into slow cooker. Add duck meat, beans and bay leaf to slow cooker. Cover and cook on low for 6 hours. Stir in marjoram, thyme and rosemary; re-cover and cook for 15 minutes longer.

 FREEZING TOMATO PASTE

Sometimes, all you need is a small amount of tomato paste rather than a full can. Here's what I do with the extra. Line a small baking sheet (or a dinner plate) with waxed paper. Spoon out large dabs of extra tomato paste onto the waxed paper; I make each one a tablespoon (15 ml) because that is a size that is often needed for recipes. Freeze until solid, then roll up the waxed paper and store it in a freezer-weight plastic food storage bag or in a plastic container. When you need a spoonful of tomato paste, just peel a frozen dab off the sheet; it will thaw very quickly.

SHREDDED DUCK ENCHILADAS

4 servings (2 per serving)
Prep: 15 minutes, plus 15 minutes before final baking in oven
Cooking: 7½ hours on low (can cook up to 8¼ hours), followed by 25 minutes in oven
Slow cooker: Standard

Here's a new way to fix duck that will appeal to anyone who enjoys Mexican-style foods. You may substitute any type of duck for the mallard; you could also use an equal amount of goose portions.

1 mallard or other wild duck (about 1¾ pounds/800 g), skin removed, cut up
1 envelope (1.25 ounce/35 g) taco seasoning mix
1 medium onion
1 fresh jalapeño pepper
2 or 3 cloves garlic
1⅔ cups (400 ml) tomato juice
8 burrito-sized flour tortillas*
1 small onion, diced
1½ cups (6 ounces/170 g/350 ml) shredded Colby-Monterey Jack cheese blend, divided

Spray inside of slow cooker with nonstick spray; set aside. Sprinkle a generous amount of taco seasoning mix over duck pieces, and rub in with your fingertips; set aside. Add remaining seasoning to slow cooker. Cut onion into quarters vertically, then slice the quarters crosswise (so you have quarter-round slices). Add to slow cooker. Remove stem and seeds from jalapeño pepper (if your skin is sensitive, wear rubber gloves when handling fresh peppers). Chop pepper and garlic together coarsely; add to slow cooker. Add juice to slow cooker; stir well, then top with seasoned duck pieces. Cover and cook on low for 7½ hours; the duck can cook as long as 8¼ hours.

When duck is ready, heat oven to 350°F (175°C). Spray 9 x 9-inch (23 x 23 cm) baking dish with nonstick spray; set aside. Use slotted spoon to transfer duck pieces to cutting board; cool slightly. Pull duck meat from bones; discard bones and any tendons (watch carefully for small rib bones and shot). Shred meat with 2 forks. Divide meat evenly between warmed flour tortillas, spooning the meat in a line across the center of each tortilla. Sprinkle onion evenly over the meat. Sprinkle about a tablespoon (15 ml) of the cheese over each tortilla. Roll tortillas up and arrange in prepared baking dish. Pour sauce from slow cooker over tortillas, spreading evenly. Top with remaining cheese. Bake until bubbly, about 25 minutes.

Flour tortillas are easier to roll if they're heated for a minute or so in the microwave; or, wrap them in foil and put them in the preheated oven for 5 to 10 minutes.

VARIATION: SHREDDED DUCK TACOS
Follow recipe above, but use only 1⅓ cups (315 ml) tomato juice. Eliminate flour tortillas; you'll need 8 hard (corn) taco shells instead. Reduce cheese to 1 cup (4 ounces/115 g/235 ml). After duck meat is cooked and shredded, return meat to sauce; cook for about 15 minutes longer, until meat is hot. Serve meat in hard taco shells, with onion, cheese and any other accompaniments you like (shredded lettuce, pickled jalapeño slices, and sliced or diced avocado work well). This is a saucy taco filling, so the best accompaniments are those that are not too wet.

ORANGE-SAUCED DUCK

4 servings
Prep: 15 minutes
Cooking: 7 to 8 hours on low
Slow cooker: Standard (see note at beginning of recipe for smaller slow cooker)

I like to serve this with hot rice and stir-fried vegetables. If you have a smaller slow cooker, prepare a single duck, cut up (or small goose, such as a snow goose). Use the same amount of sauce; leftovers are great spooned over rice.

1 small orange, well washed
2 whole wild mallards or other medium-sized ducks, skin on or removed
Salt and pepper
½ cup (120 ml) orange juice
¼ cup (60 ml) port wine or sweet vermouth
¼ cup (60 ml) currant jelly
2 tablespoons (30 ml) cornstarch
½ teaspoon (2.5 ml) dry mustard powder
½ teaspoon (2.5 ml) chopped fresh tarragon, optional

Slice orange and arrange slices in bottom of slow cooker. Sprinkle ducks generously inside and out with salt and pepper; arrange on top of orange slices, breast-side up. In small saucepan, combine orange juice, wine, jelly, cornstarch, mustard and tarragon. Cook over medium heat, stirring constantly, until sauce thickens and bubbles, about 5 minutes. Spoon about half of the sauce over the ducks; refrigerate saucepan with remaining sauce. Cover slow cooker and cook until tender, 7 to 8 hours on low; the meat will start to separate from the bone when it is done. Transfer ducks to serving platter. Strain juices from slow cooker into saucepan with reserved sauce; discard orange slices. Heat sauce over medium heat, stirring frequently, until hot. Season to taste with salt and pepper. Serve sauce with ducks.

VARIATION:

This is for those who really love the tangy-sweet flavor of oranges with their duck. Follow recipe above, adding 1 can (11 ounces/312 g) mandarin oranges, drained, to the sauce during final heating.

DUCK OR GOOSE AND DRESSING

6 servings
Prep: 15 minutes
Cooking: 7 1/2 hours on low, or 4 hours on high (can cook up to 8 hours on low)
Slow cooker: Standard

Dried apricots give this dish an unexpected touch that goes great with the waterfowl.

1 tablespoon (15 g/15 ml) butter or stick margarine
2 ribs celery, diced
Half of a medium onion, diced
1 pound (454 g) boneless, skinless duck or goose meat, cut into small bite-sized pieces
1 package (14 ounces/397 g) herb-seasoned cubed stuffing mix
2 cups (475 ml) chicken broth
4 ounces (115 g) dried apricots, diced
For serving: Prepared gravy

Spray inside of slow cooker with nonstick spray; set aside. In Dutch oven, melt butter over medium heat. Add celery and onion; cook, stirring occasionally, until tender-crisp, about 5 minutes. Remove from heat. Add duck or goose, stuffing, broth and apricots; stir well to mix. Transfer mixture to prepared slow cooker. Cover and cook on low for 7 1/2 hours, or on high for 4 hours; stuffing can cook up to 8 hours on low. Just before serving, prepare gravy from packaged mix, or heat gravy from a jar. Serve dressing with hot gravy.

 TIPS TO MAKE CLEANUP EASIER

During the long cooking time, foods tend to bake onto the crock, especially at the surface of the food. After you've filled the crock with food, take a damp paper towel and wipe off any sauce or liquid that may have slopped up around the rim and inside the crock above the food; this prevents it from getting baked on. Once the meal has been served, fill the crock with warm, soapy water and let it sit for an hour or so, then use a nylon net pad to scrub off any caked-on gunk; don't use metal scrubbers, as they can scratch the surface. The crock should now come clean in the dishwasher, or can be washed by hand.

If your stoneware crock develops mineral marks over time (like a hard-water ring), fill it three-quarters full with hot water, then add 1 cup (240 ml) white vinegar. Cover and cook on high for 2 hours. Let the crock cool before washing.

CHAPTER FIVE

PARTY TIME

Con Queso Dip

Homemade Venison Salami

Manhattan-Style Wild Boar or Javelina Chunks

Those Tiny Meatballs

Party Nachos with Venison

Venison Pâté

Hot Spiced Wine

Sausage Snacks

Simmering Spice Potpourri

Venison Sausage Pizza Dip

Mulled Cranberry-Apple Cider

Con Queso Dip

10 servings
Prep: 15 minutes
Cooking: 2 to 3 hours on low (can cook up to 5 hours on low)
Slow cooker: Mini or Personal

If you have a larger slow cooker (or if you're making party fixings for a crowd), simply double the ingredients.

8 ounces (225 g) uncooked venison sausage (remove casings if links)
   or plain ground venison
1 loaf (1 pound/454 g) pasteurized-process cheese such as Velveeta
1 cup (235 ml) chunky-style salsa
1 to 2 teaspoons (5 to 10 ml) taco seasoning mix or chili powder blend

*Accompaniments: **Tortilla chips, bagel chips or crackers***

In medium skillet, cook sausage over medium heat, stirring frequently to break up, until meat is no longer pink and the texture is fine. Drain and discard drippings. Spray inside of slow cooker with non-stick spray. Dice cheese and add to slow cooker, along with cooked sausage, salsa and seasoning. Cover and cook on low for 2 to 3 hours or until cheese melts and mixture is hot, stirring several times; dip can cook as long as 5 hours. Stir again just before serving. Serve with chips or crackers.

---

 3 SLOW-COOKER SAFETY TIPS

Slow cookers are safe appliances—when used correctly. Here are 3 safety tips to keep in mind; you should also review the Use and Care information that may have come with your slow cooker when you purchased it.

• *Ensure that the cord isn't hanging over the edge of a countertop, where it may be snagged by children or pets.*

• *When the dish is ready, you may remove the crock from the base with hot pads and carry it to the table for serving; however, if you're serving family-style, it may be safer to leave the crock inside the base unit, to avoid spills while carrying.*

• *Never immerse the base in water; if it becomes dirty, wipe it with a damp rag.*

HOMEMADE VENISON SALAMI

1 salami (about 1 pound/454 g)
Prep: 15 minutes, plus 24 hours refrigeration
Cooking: 3 hours on high
Slow cooker: Standard or Large, oval

Here's an easy way to make homemade salami. Feel free to vary the spices to suit your taste, but don't substitute another type of salt for the Morton Tender Quick curing salt; it contains a curing agent that is essential to safe salami.

1 pound (454 g) ground venison
¹⁄₂ cup (120 ml) sweet vermouth or apple juice
4¹⁄₂ teaspoons (22.5 ml) Morton Tender Quick curing salt*
2 teaspoons (10 ml) paprika (use hot paprika for extra kick, if you like)
1 teaspoon (5 ml) whole mustard seeds
¹⁄₂ teaspoon (2.5 ml) liquid smoke
¹⁄₄ teaspoon (1.25 ml) cracked black pepper
1 clove garlic, pressed or minced

You'll also need: Cheesecloth, kitchen string, foil, loaf pan that fits completely inside slow cooker**

In nonreactive mixing bowl (glass, ceramic or stainless steel), combine all ingredients and mix well with your hands. Cover and refrigerate for 24 hours.

After 24 hours, you'll be ready to shape and cook the salami. Begin heating a pan of water to boiling. Shape the venison mixture into a roll that is about 2¹⁄₂ to 3 inches (6.25 to 7.5 cm) in diameter, and just a bit shorter than your loaf pan. Wrap in doubled cheesecloth, twisting the ends against the meat. Tie ends tightly with kitchen string. Make 4 foil "logs" that are the width of the loaf pan and about ³⁄₄ inch (2 cm) high; arrange the logs inside the bottom of the loaf pan. Place the wrapped meat on the logs. Cover top of loaf pan tightly with foil. Place loaf pan in slow cooker. Add boiling water, pouring carefully along the side of the slow cooker, to come about halfway up the sides of the loaf pan (if using a foil loaf pan, it may float; weight top with heavy saucer). Cover slow cooker and cook on high for 3 hours. Transfer roll to a plate and refrigerate for at least 12 hours before slicing. This salami will keep for about a week in the refrigerator; freeze for longer storage.

*Morton TenderQuick Curing Salt is usually found in the seasonings aisle with canning/pickling salt. It is used for sausage making, as well as for brining fish and jerky prior to smoking.

**If a standard-sized loaf pan is too big for your slow cooker (due to the handles), look for foil loaf pans in the baking aisle of the supermarket. Get the largest that will fit completely inside your slow cooker. For more information, read the first paragraph of Venison Pâté on page 111.

MANHATTAN-STYLE WILD BOAR OR JAVELINA CHUNKS

6 to 8 appetizer servings
Prep: 15 minutes
Cooking: 2 hours on low (can cook up to 4 hours)
Slow cooker: Small or Standard

This adults-only appetizer uses the basic ingredients of a Manhattan cocktail, combined with wild boar or javelina, for an unusual party dish.

2 pounds (900 g) boneless wild boar or javelina chops,
    well trimmed before weighing
Salt
2 tablespoons (30 g/30 ml) butter, divided
1 tablespoon (15 ml) vegetable oil
¾ cup (180 ml) bourbon or blended whiskey
⅜ cup (90 ml) sweet vermouth
2 teaspoons (10 ml) sugar
4 generous dashes Angostura bitters (from liquor store,
    or in bar-mix area of a supermarket)
1 tablespoon (15 ml) cornstarch
15 maraschino cherries, stems removed, halved
1 tablespoon (15 ml) juice from the maraschino cherries

Cut boar into 1-inch (2.5 cm) cubes; salt generously. In large skillet, melt half of the butter in the oil over medium heat. Add half of the boar chunks; increase heat to medium-high and brown on all sides. Use tongs to transfer boar to slow cooker. Add remaining butter to skillet, and brown remaining boar chunks. Transfer boar to slow cooker. Add bourbon, vermouth, sugar and bitters to skillet, stirring to loosen any browned bits. Cook over low heat for about 10 minutes. Blend in cornstarch. Pour bourbon mixture into slow cooker. Add cherries and cherry juice. Cover and cook on low for 2 hours; the mixture can cook for as long as 4 hours. If your slow cooker has a "keep warm" setting, turn setting to that after mixture is completely hot; this will prevent overcooking.

THOSE TINY MEATBALLS

8 to 10 appetizer servings
Prep: 45 minutes
Cooking: 4 hours on low, or 2 hours on high (can cook up to 6 hours on low)
Slow cooker: Standard

Always a hit at any party, these will be among the first dishes to disappear. You'll find the chili sauce in the supermarket next to the ketchup.

1 egg
¹⁄₃ cup (80 ml) seasoned bread crumbs
¹⁄₂ teaspoon (2.5 ml) garlic salt
1 bottle (12 ounces/340 g) chili sauce such as Heinz
1 jar (10 ounces/284 g) grape jelly
1 tablespoon (15 ml) Worcestershire sauce
1¹⁄₂ pounds (680 g) ground venison

Heat oven to 375°F/190°C. In large mixing bowl, beat egg with fork. Stir in bread crumbs, add garlic and salt; let stand for 5 minutes. In slow cooker, combine chili sauce, jelly and Worcestershire sauce; stir to mix well and set aside. Add ground venison to mixing bowl with egg; mix well with your hands.

Shape into 1-inch (2.5 cm) meatballs, placing in 10 x 15-inch (25 x 38 cm) baking dish. Bake until meatballs are no longer pink, about 15 minutes. Use tongs to transfer meatballs to slow cooker; discard drippings. Cover slow cooker and cook on low for 4 hours, or on high for 2 hours, stirring once or twice; meatballs can cook on low up to 6 hours. If your slow cooker has a "keep warm" setting, turn setting to that after meatballs and sauce are completely hot; this will prevent overcooking. If the sauce gets too thick after a while, stir in a bit of hot water.

VARIATION: TANGY SAUSAGES

Follow recipe above, but eliminate egg, bread crumbs, garlic salt and venison. Prepare sauce as directed. Slice 2 pounds (900 g) smoked, fully-cooked venison sausages into 1-inch (2.5 cm) pieces; add to sauce. Cover and cook on low for 4 hours, or on high for 2 hours, as directed. If you like, you could also add 1 can (8 ounces/227 g) pineapple chunks, drained, to the sauce along with the sliced sausages.

BUFFET TIPS

The slow cooker works great for buffets; you can serve the food right out of the crock, and if you leave the slow cooker plugged in (turned to "keep warm"), the food will remain warm throughout even the longest meal. But did you know that you can use the slow cooker to keep other foods warm—even those that weren't prepared in it?

To ensure safety, remember that the food must be hot when it goes into the slow cooker; and for best results, the slow cooker should be preheated. To preheat the slow cooker, either fill it with water and turn it to high for an hour or two; or, fill it with boiling water and let stand for 10 minutes. Drain the water, and carefully wipe the inside dry. Then, fill the preheated slow cooker with hot, freshly prepared food such as mashed potatoes, stuffing or vegetables. Turn the slow cooker to "keep warm" (or low, if your slow cooker doesn't have a warm setting), and keep it plugged in for the duration of the meal. Note that the slow cooker should never be used to re-heat foods, only to hold foods that are already hot.

PARTY NACHOS WITH VENISON

8 to 10 servings
Prep: 15 minutes, plus 15 minutes just prior to serving
Cooking: 8 hours on low, or 4 hours on high (can cook up to 9 hours on low)
Slow cooker: Small or Standard

1 can (15 ounces/425 g) chili beans, undrained
2 pounds (900 g) venison steaks
1 envelope (1.25 ounces/35 g) taco seasoning mix
1 can (14½ ounces/411 g) diced tomatoes, drained
**For serving: Tortilla chips, shredded Monterey Jack cheese, sour cream, salsa, sliced
pickled jalapeño peppers, diced tomatoes, diced onions, shredded lettuce**

Spread undrained beans in slow cooker. Top with steaks; sprinkle taco seasoning evenly over meat. Top with tomatoes. Cover and cook on low for 8 hours, or on high for 4 hours; mixture can cook on low for as long as 9 hours. Transfer meat to cutting board; cool slightly. While meat is cooling, use potato masher to mash beans in slow cooker. Use two forks to shred meat apart on cutting board; discard any bones or tough material. Return shredded meat to slow cooker; stir well.

To serve, each guest places some tortilla chips on a plate, then tops the chips with a scoop of the meat mixture and adds toppings as desired. The meat mixture can sit in the slow cooker on low for up to 2 hours (stir occasionally).

VARIATION: DUCK OR GOOSE NACHOS
Substitute 2 pounds (900 g) boneless, skinless goose or duck (or 2½ to 3 pounds/1.125 to 1.35 kg bone-in thighs) for the venison steaks. Proceed as directed; total cooking time may be slightly less.

VENISON PÂTÉ

10 appetizer servings
Prep: 30 minutes
Cooking: 2 ¾ hours on high
  (Note: Cooked pâté must be refrigerated overnight before serving)
Slow cooker: Large oval slow cooker, or medium roaster

Here's an elegant appetizer or first course that no one will believe was prepared in a slow cooker! Serve with grainy mustard, French bread and pickled onions.

⅓ cup (80 ml) brandy
6 whole prunes
8 or 9 slices bacon
Half of a small onion
3 cloves garlic
1 pound (454 g) boneless venison chops,
  steaks or roast, well trimmed
  before weighing
1 pound (454 g) boneless country-style
  pork ribs or other moderately fatty cut

¼ cup (60 ml) red wine
1 tablespoon (15 ml) whole mustard seeds
1 teaspoon (5 ml) dried thyme leaves
1 teaspoon (5 ml) coarsely ground
  black pepper
1 teaspoon (5 ml) salt
¼ cup (60 ml/35 g) coarsely chopped
  pistachios or blanched almonds
You'll also need: Standard-sized loaf pan,
  foil, clean garden brick

The loaf pan doesn't have to sit on the bottom of the slow cooker, but it does have to fit inside enough to allow the lid to fit snugly. Before beginning, test the loaf pan in your equipment. If there is a gap between the bottom of the loaf pan and the bottom of the slow cooker (as is the case with my 6-quart Rival Crockpot), roll up two loose balls of foil about the size of softballs, then place them into the slow cooker. Place the loaf pan on top of the foil, pressing gently until it sits level. Double-check that the lid still fits snugly, and press the foil balls down a bit more until the lid fits properly. (If you are using a roaster or a very large slow cooker that allows the loaf pan to sit on the bottom of the cooking vessel, make two foil ropes that will prop the loaf pan up slightly off the bottom; for the roaster, you'll be cooking inside the insert.)

In small saucepan, heat brandy over low heat until hot but not boiling. Stir in prunes; remove from heat and set aside. Line loaf pan with bacon slices by placing 4 or 5 slices (as needed to cover) cross-wise on the bottom and up the sides, allowing excess to hang over the sides. Cut 2 bacon slices in half crosswise, and place 2 halves up each end of the pan. Set aside remaining 2 slices. Begin heating a large pot of water to boiling; you'll need several quarts (several liters) of boiling water.

Add onion and garlic to food processor fitted with metal chopping blade; pulse on-and-off until medium-fine. Cut venison and pork into 1-inch (2.5 cm) cubes. Add to food processor with onion; pulse on-and-off until chopped to medium consistency (more coarse than hamburger; see sidebar on page 46 for more information on chopping meat in a food processor). In mixing bowl, combine chopped meat mixture with wine, mustard seeds, thyme, pepper and salt. Mix gently but thoroughly with your hands, picking out and discarding any stringy silverskin you might find. Pack half of the meat mixture into prepared loaf pan. Drain prunes, discarding brandy. Arrange prunes along the center of the chopped meat in the loaf pan; sprinkle pistachios over meat. Top with remaining meat, pressing down firmly. Fold bacon ends over top of meat. Place 2 remaining bacon slices on top of loaf, cutting to the

continued on page 113

length of the loaf pan and tucking the cut ends wherever they seem to fit. Cover loaf pan with foil, using enough to wrap almost to the bottom of the pan. Press foil onto bacon on top and seal well around the edges.

Place the filled, foil-wrapped loaf pan on top of the foil balls (or ropes), pressing until the loaf pan sits level. Carefully pour boiling water into the unplugged slow cooker to come halfway up the sides of the loaf pan (pour the water along the edge so it doesn't hit the top of the loaf, and be very careful to avoid splashing water onto yourself). Mop up any spilled water, checking to be sure that the plug and cord of the slow cooker are dry before plugging it in. Cover and cook on high for 2¾ hours (if you're using a roaster, set it to 325°F/164°C). After cooking, unplug the slow cooker. Carefully remove loaf pan from slow cooker. I use a wooden spatula to lift the loaf pan from underneath, then grab it with potholders; it's hot, and the water will be boiling, so take great care and get someone to help you if possible. Allow to cool, still wrapped, for an hour at room temperature. Place a foil-wrapped brick on top of foil-wrapped loaf pan; refrigerate overnight.

To serve, remove foil. Pour out and discard any juices from the loaf pan. Use a table knife to loosen around edges of pâté; if it seems stuck, hold the loaf pan up to its rim in a sink of very hot water for a minute to loosen the pâté. Invert onto plate. Scrape away any loose fat or gelatinous juices. Slice into 10 pieces for serving. Note: The bacon may look raw, but it is completely cooked and is considered an important part of the pâté. You may wish to slice off a thin piece on each end to eliminate the solid layer of bacon slices on the end pieces.

Hot Spiced Wine

8 to 10 servings
Prep: 15 minutes
Cooking: 2 hours on low, or 1 hour on high (can cook up to 3 hours on low)
Slow cooker: Any that holds at least 2.5 quarts (2.5 liters): Personal, Small or Standard

Start a batch of this an hour or two in advance of a party, and let it simmer away until guests arrive. You might want to offer a plate of orange and lemon slices, so guests can float one in their cup.

2 cups (475 ml) water
3 tea bags
½ cup (125 ml/100 g) sugar
1 bottle (750 ml) cabernet sauvignon
　　or other dry, medium-bodied red wine

1 cup (235 ml) dark rum
1 can (6 ounces/177 ml) frozen
　　orange juice concentrate, thawed
3 whole cloves
1 stick cinnamon

In saucepan or tea kettle, heat water to boiling. Remove from heat; immediately add tea bags and let steep for 5 to 10 minutes. Remove and discard tea bags. Add sugar to tea; stir until sugar dissolves. Add sweetened tea and remaining ingredients to slow cooker, stirring to blend. Cover and cook on low for 2 hours, or on high for 1 hour; the mixture can cook on low for up to 3 hours. You can also turn the slow cooker to the "warm" setting once the mixture is hot; it will be fine for several hours.

SAUSAGE SNACKS

12 appetizer servings
Prep: 15 minutes
Cooking: 4 hours on low, or 2 hours on high (can cook up to 6 hours on low)
Slow cooker: Small or Standard

Your favorite barbecue sauce pairs up with a few simple pantry ingredients to form a tasty sauce for venison sausages.

1 bottle (18 ounces/510 g) barbecue sauce
1 can (9 ounces/255 g) bean dip
1 small onion, minced
1 clove garlic, pressed or finely minced
¼ cup (60 ml/55 g) packed brown sugar

2 tablespoons (30 ml) cider vinegar
1 tablespoon (15 ml) prepared mustard
2 pounds (900 g) smoked,
 fully cooked venison sausage links

In slow cooker, stir together all ingredients except sausages; if the barbecue sauce you use is particularly thick, you may want to add a bit of water. Cut the sausages into 1-inch (2.5 cm) pieces; add to sauce. Cover and cook on low for 4 hours, or on high for 2 hours, stirring once or twice; this can remain on low for as long as 6 hours. If your slow cooker has a "keep warm" setting, turn setting to that after sausage and sauce are completely hot; this will prevent overcooking. If the sauce gets too thick after a while, stir in a bit of hot water.

SIMMERING SPICE POTPOURRI

Inedible; for fragrance only
Prep: 15 minutes
Heating time: 2 hours on high, or 3 to 4 hours on low; can simmer on low for many hours
Slow cooker: Mini (to prepare in Personal-sized slow cooker, simply double the ingredients)

Have a batch of this going before guests arrive for a party; your whole house will smell great!

1½ cups (350 ml) hot water
1 teaspoon (5 ml) vanilla extract
1 teaspoon (5 ml) cinnamon
¼ teaspoon (1.25 ml) nutmeg
Peel from half of an orange, cut off in thin strips

Combine all ingredients in slow cooker. Cover and heat on high for 2 hours, or on low for 3 to 4 hours. Once the mixture is hot, set the lid ajar on the slow cooker so some steam escapes; reduce heat to low if necessary. The potpourri can be left to simmer on low for many hours; check to be sure that the water isn't evaporating, and replenish if necessary. Be sure to tell your guests that this mixture isn't to be consumed; it wouldn't hurt them, but it probably won't taste very good!

VENISON SAUSAGE PIZZA DIP

12 appetizer servings
Prep: 15 minutes
Cooking: 6 hours on low, or 3 hours on high (can cook up to 8 hours on low)
Slow cooker: Small or Standard

Offer a basket of breadsticks, pita wedges or bread chunks to accompany this spicy dip.

1 pound (454 g) uncooked venison sausage (remove casings if links)
1 small onion, minced
Half of a green or red bell pepper, diced
1 jar (26 ounces/1 pound 10 ounces/737 g) marinara or other prepared pasta sauce
2 teaspoons (10 ml) dried Italian herb blend (or a mix of oregano and basil)

¼ teaspoon (1.25 ml) hot red pepper flakes, or to taste
1 can (4¼ ounces/120 g) chopped black olives, drained
¼ cup (30 g/60 ml) shredded Parmesan cheese

In large skillet, cook sausage over medium heat, stirring frequently to break up, until some of the fat is rendered. Add onion and bell pepper and continue to cook, stirring frequently, until meat is no longer pink and vegetables are tender-crisp, about 5 minutes. Drain and discard excess grease; transfer mixture to slow cooker. Add pasta sauce, herbs and pepper flakes; stir well. Cover and cook on low for 6 hours, or on high for 3 hours; the dip can cook up to 8 hours on low. Just before serving, stir in olives and Parmesan cheese. If your slow cooker has a "keep warm" setting, turn setting to that after adding the olives and cheese; this will prevent overcooking. If the dip gets too thick after a while, stir in a bit of hot water.

MULLED CRANBERRY-APPLE CIDER

12 servings
Prep: 15 minutes
Cooking: 4 hours on low, or 2 hours on high (can cook up to 7 hours on low)
Slow cooker: Small or Standard

This delicious beverage serves two purposes: It provides a delicious warmer for a fall or winter party, and it makes your kitchen smell great.

1 quart (1 liter) processed apple cider (not the refrigerated kind)
1 quart (1 liter) cranberry juice cocktail
1 cup (235 ml) brandy, optional
1 orange, well washed, thinly sliced

2 whole cinnamon sticks
4 slices peeled fresh gingerroot, each about ¼ inch (6 mm) thick
10 whole cloves
½ cup (120 ml) honey

Combine all ingredients in slow cooker. Cover and cook on low for 4 hours, or on high for 2 hours; mixture can cook on low for as long as 7 hours. Serve hot.

CHAPTER SIX

ON THE SIDE

SCALLOPED TWO-COLOR POTATOES

6 servings
Prep: 15 minutes
Cooking: 7 hours on low, or 3 1/2 hours on high (can cook up to 8 hours on low)
Slow cooker: Standard

This classic side dish get jazzed up with the addition of orange-fleshed sweet potatoes (which are often called yams; see below). A food processor helps with the slicing chores.

2 pounds (1 kg) russet potatoes (about 3 large)
1 1/2 pounds (675 g) orange-fleshed sweet potatoes (see sidebar; about 3 medium)
1 small onion
2 teaspoons (10 ml) vegetable oil
1 1/2 cups (6 ounces/170 g/350 ml) shredded Swiss cheese
Celery salt, seasoned salt or plain salt

Pepper
1 can (12 ounces/354 ml) evaporated milk (reduced-fat works fine)
1/4 cup (35 g) all-purpose flour
2 tablespoons (30 g/30 ml) butter or stick margarine, cut up
1/2 cup (65 g/120 ml) shredded Parmesan cheese
Paprika for garnish, optional

Peel russet and sweet potatoes, and slice to medium thickness; set aside. Peel onion, and slice thinly. Grease slow cooker liberally with the oil. Arrange one-third of the russet potato slices in slow cooker; top with one-third of the sweet potatoes, half of the onions and one-third of the Swiss cheese. Sprinkle with salt and pepper to taste. Repeat layers twice, ending with Swiss cheese. In mixing bowl, whisk together milk and flour. Pour evenly over potatoes. Distribute cut-up butter evenly over the top; sprinkle with Parmesan cheese. Sprinkle lightly with paprika. Cover and cook on low for 7 hours, or on high for 3 1/2 hours; the potatoes can cook up to 8 hours on low.

"YAMS" VERSUS SWEET POTATOES

If you visit the produce section of the supermarket, chances are good you'll see several types of sweet potatoes, including some that are labeled "yams." Actually, the true yam is botanically unrelated to sweet potatoes. You may find true yams ("tropical yams") at a Latin market, but they are quite different from the "yams" we're used to using; they have firm, dry, bland flesh that is light in color.

The "regular" sweet potato has medium-colored flesh that is relatively dry and mealy—somewhat like a russet potato (also called an Idaho potato or baking potato). "Garnet yams," "Jersey yams," and "jewel yams" are sweet potatoes that have darker, moister flesh than the "regular" sweet potatoes; they tend to hold together better in stews. The skins on these "yams" is also usually darker than that of the regular sweet potato. In this book, I refer to these "yams" as orange-fleshed sweet potatoes.

COUNTRY-STYLE PASTA CASSEROLE

6 to 8 servings
Prep: 15 minutes
Cooking: 4 hours on low, or 2 hours on high
Slow cooker: Standard

8 ounces (225 g) uncooked egg-noodle
    dumplings (large, wavy egg noodles)
4 slices bacon, cut up
1½ cups (350 ml/340 g) sour cream
    (reduced-fat works fine)
1½ cups (350 ml) cottage cheese
    with chives

⅓ cup (80 ml/45 g) all-purpose flour
1 teaspoon (5 ml) garlic salt
¼ teaspoon (1.25 ml) Tabasco sauce
1 jar (2 ounces/57 g) diced
    pimientos, drained

Spray inside of slow cooker generously with nonstick spray; set aside. Heat a large pot of salted water to boiling. Add noodles and cook until not quite tender; they should still be fairly firm in the middle (the noodles will get additional cooking in the slow cooker). While noodles are cooking, cook bacon in medium skillet over medium heat until crisp, stirring frequently. When noodles are cooked, drain and return to cooking pot. Use slotted spoon to transfer cooked bacon to pot with noodles; stir to mix together (the drippings clinging to the bacon prevent the noodles from sticking together).

In large mixing bowl, combine remaining ingredients, stirring to blend in flour. Add noodle mixture, stirring to combine. Transfer mixture to prepared slow cooker. Cover and cook on low for 4 hours, or on high for 2 hours.

BUTTERMILK AND BACON POTATOES

6 servings
Prep: 15 minutes
Cooking: 6½ to 7 hours on low, or 3 to 3½ hours on high (can cook up to 8 hours on low)
Slow cooker: Standard or Large

This is a very rich side dish; serve it with a simple roast.

1 can (10¾ ounces/305 g)
    condensed cream of celery
    soup (reduced-fat works fine)
½ cup (120 ml) bottled buttermilk-
    ranch dressing
6 slices bacon, cut up

Half of a small onion, sliced into
    half rings
2 pounds (1 kg) small red or
    Yukon gold potatoes, washed
    but unpeeled

continued on page 119

Spray inside of slow cooker with nonstick spray. Add soup and dressing, stirring to combine; set aside. In large skillet, cook bacon over medium heat, stirring frequently, until bacon is just crisp. Add onion; cook for about 5 minutes longer, stirring occasionally. Meanwhile, slice potatoes ⅜ inch (9 mm) thick, adding to slow cooker as you go. When bacon mixture has cooked as directed, use slotted spoon to transfer to slow cooker; discard drippings. Stir everything together gently with a wooden spoon. Cover and cook until potatoes are tender, 6½ to 7 hours on low or 3 to 3½ hours on high; potatoes can cook up to 8 hours on low.

GERMAN-STYLE POTATO SALAD

5 or 6 servings
Prep: 15 minutes
Cooking: 7 hours on low, or 4 hours on high (can cook up to 8 hours on low)
Slow cooker: Standard

Use pepper bacon for extra kick, if you like.

¼ **pound (115 g) thick-sliced bacon, cut up**
1 **small white onion, diced**
2 **ribs celery, diced**
2 **pounds (900 g) red-skinned potatoes,**
   washed but unpeeled
½ **cup (120 ml) cider vinegar or**
   rice vinegar
½ **cup (120 ml) water**
¼ **cup (60 ml/50 g) sugar**

2 **tablespoons (30 ml) juice from**
   a jar of pickles
1 **tablespoon (15 ml) cornstarch**
1 **teaspoon (5 ml) salt**
1 **teaspoon (5 ml) dry mustard powder**
½ **teaspoon (2.5 ml) celery seed**
Optional garnishes: Sliced hard-cooked
   eggs, sliced radishes,
   chopped fresh parsley

In large skillet, cook bacon over medium heat until just crisp, stirring frequently. Drain and discard all but about 1 tablespoon (15 ml) drippings. Add onion and celery; cook until tender-crisp, stirring occasionally. Meanwhile, slice potatoes about ¼ inch (6 mm) thick; place in slow cooker. Combine remaining ingredients except garnishes in measuring cup or bowl; stir well to blend in cornstarch and sugar, then add to slow cooker with potatoes. When vegetables are tender-crisp, scrape into slow cooker, then stir gently with a wooden spoon to combine. Cover and cook on low for 7 hours, or on high for 4 hours, until potatoes are tender; the potatoes can cook up to 8 hours on low. Turn slow cooker off; if your crock is removable, take it out of the base and set aside to cool slightly. Garnish potatoes with sliced eggs and radishes; sprinkle with chopped parsley.

Baked Beans with Ham

8 to 10 servings
Prep: Overnight soaking, plus 30 minutes before cooking
  and 15 minutes shortly before serving
Cooking: 9 to 10 hours on low
Slow cooker: Standard or Large

These baked beans are fairly sweet; reduce the molasses a bit if you prefer beans that are less sweet. The beans will be cooked after 9 hours, but they get better with the additional hour of cooking.

1 pound (454 g) dry navy beans, picked over
1 teaspoon (5 ml) vegetable oil
1 medium onion, chopped
1 can (8 ounces/227g) tomato sauce
¾ cup (180 ml) molasses
¼ cup (60 ml/55 g) packed brown sugar
1 tablespoon (15 ml) Worcestershire sauce
1½ teaspoons (7.5 ml) dry mustard powder
¼ teaspoon (1.25 ml) pepper
½ cup (120 ml) water, approximate
Ham hock (12 to 16 ounces/340 to 454 g)

Soak beans overnight, or use the quick-soak method (see sidebar on page 121). When beans are ready for cooking, drain and rinse in cold water. Return beans to pot; add enough fresh water to cover by an inch. Heat to boiling over medium-high heat; boil gently for 10 minutes. Drain and rinse.

While beans are boiling, prepare other ingredients. Brush inside of slow cooker with oil. Add onion, tomato sauce, molasses, brown sugar, Worcestershire sauce, mustard powder and pepper to slow cooker. When beans have been boiled, drained and rinsed, add to slow cooker; stir well. Add enough water to come just to the level of the beans. Nestle ham hock into beans. Cover and cook until beans are tender, 9 to 10 hours on low. Remove ham hock and set aside to cool slightly. If bean mixture is too thin, remove about a cup and mash with potato masher; return to pot, stirring in well. Pick meat from cooled ham hock; discard bones, fat and any skin. Return ham meat to beans; stir well.

VARIATION: ZIPPY BAKED BEANS WITH HAM
Follow recipe above, substituting 1 cup (235 ml) of your favorite spicy barbecue sauce for the tomato sauce. Proceed as directed.

VARIATION: BAKED BEANS WITH VENISON SAUSAGE
Omit ham hock; assemble and cook beans for 8 hours. After 8 hours, slice ¾ pound (340 g) of smoked, fully cooked venison sausages into lengthwise quarters; cut quarters into ¼-inch (6 mm) pieces. Stir into beans. Re-cover and continue cooking as directed.

EASY RICE PILAF

6 servings
Prep: 15 minutes
Cooking: 1½ to 2 hours on high
Slow cooker: Small or Standard

This sweet and nutty pilaf is easy to put together a few hours before dinner. It goes particularly well with a simple venison roast, or with roast duck, goose, pheasant or turkey.

Half of a small onion, diced
1 rib celery, diced
¼ cup (60 ml/20 g) diced dried apple slices
¼ cup (60 ml/25 g) diced dried apricots
1 box (7 ounces/198 g) white-and-wild-rice blend*

2 cups (475 ml) water*
1 tablespoon (15 g/15 ml) butter or stick margarine
¼ cup (60 ml/26 g) coarsely chopped pecans or walnuts

In slow cooker, combine onion, celery, apple, apricots and rice blend (including seasoning). In saucepan, combine water and butter; heat to boiling over high heat. Pour boiling water into slow cooker; stir to blend. Cover and cook on high until rice is tender and liquid is absorbed, 1½ to 2 hours. Just before serving, stir in pecans.

*This recipe was tested with Zatarain's New Orleans Style Long Grain & Wild Rice. If you're using a different type, you may need to adjust the amount of water needed. The Zatarain's mix calls for 2¼ cups (530 ml) water, with a cooking time of 25 minutes. Because water doesn't evaporate in the slow cooker, the water should be reduced slightly; here, it was reduced from 2¼ to 2 cups (530 ml to 475 ml). Note that this technique is not intended for use with "quick-cook" rice blends.

VARIATION: EASY RICE PILAF WITH SAUSAGE

For a more substantial dish, cook ¼ pound (113 g) breakfast-style sausage (pork or venison) in a skillet over medium heat until no longer pink, stirring to break up. Drain; add sausage to slow cooker with rice and other ingredients, and proceed as directed.

 USING DRY BEANS IN THE SLOW COOKER

Dry beans always need soaking before using them in slow-cooker recipes. Rinse and pick over the beans, tossing any stones or other foreign material you may find. Place beans in a large pot. Cover with 2 inches (5 cm) of water. Here are two methods:

• For the overnight method, simply let the beans soak overnight before draining and rinsing them; they are now ready to use in a recipe.

• For the quick-soak method, heat pot of water and beans to boiling. Reduce heat and cook at a very gentle boil for about 5 minutes. Remove from heat and let stand 1 hour. Drain and rinse beans; they are now ready for use in a recipe.

Dry beans are best when they are fresh; older beans that have been laying around the store shelf or in your cupboard for a year or more may never become tender. Buy beans from a store that has a good turnover (rather than from a convenience store, for example, where beans may sit on the shelf for a long time).

EASY ACORN SQUASH

2 servings
Prep: 15 minutes
Cooking: 3 to 3¼ hours on high, or 6 to 7 hours on low
Slow cooker: Standard or Large

Here's an easy side dish that comes out tender and tasty. Feel free to use any type of seasoned salt or pepper that you like in place of the plain salt and pepper.

1 cup (235 ml) hot water
1 acorn squash (about 1¼ pounds/570 g)
2 tablespoons (30 g/30 ml) butter or stick margarine, divided
1 tablespoon (15 ml) packed brown sugar, divided
3 tablespoons (45 ml/25 g) craisins, divided
Salt and pepper

Add water to slow cooker. Break off stem from squash if necessary. Using a large knife, carefully cut squash in half from top to bottom (it's easiest to do this with the squash lying on its side on the cutting board; cut between the natural ribs, taking care so the knife doesn't slip). Scoop out and discard the seeds and strings. Place squash halves, cut-side up, in slow cooker. Divide butter evenly between the 2 halves, following with the sugar and craisins. Sprinkle squash generously with salt and pepper. Cover and cook until squash is very tender, 3 to 3¼ hours on high or 6 to 7 hours on low. To serve, use two large spoons to remove each squash half from the slow cooker, taking care not to collapse the shell. Serve squash in the shell, or scoop out into a serving dish if you prefer.

VARIATION: SAVORY STUFFED ACORN SQUASH

Add water to slow cooker as directed. Cut and hollow squash as directed; place in slow cooker. Eliminate butter; reduce brown sugar to 1 tablespoon (15 ml), but don't put it into the squash halves at this time. In medium skillet over medium heat, brown 4 ounces (115 g) uncooked venison sausage (casings removed if links), until meat loses its pink color. Add half of a small onion, chopped, and cook until onion is tender-crisp. Remove from heat. Stir in the craisins. Divide filling mixture evenly between squash halves. Top filling with evenly divided brown sugar. Sprinkle with salt and pepper. Cook as directed.

PROTECT YOUR COUNTERTOPS!

Slow cookers can wreak havoc with countertops—especially solid-surface countertops such as Corian®. Both the base and the crock will scratch countertops, so it's a good idea to place them on a cutting board rather than directly on the countertop. Slow cookers also produce a fair amount of heat, which can damage solid-surface and other countertops. A wooden cutting board, hot-pot trivet, or a thick heat-proof mat will prevent any marking or softening of the countertop. Always keep towels and other easily flammable materials away from the slow cooker.

SLOW-COOKER DRESSING

8 to 10 servings
Prep: 30 minutes
Cooking: 4 hours on low, or 2 hours on high (can cook up to 5 hours on low)
Slow cooker: Standard or Large

When the oven is bursting at the seams during holiday time, prepare this delicious dressing in the slow cooker.

8 ounces (225 g) uncooked venison sausage
  (casings removed if links)
3 ribs celery, sliced
1 medium onion, diced
1 cup (235 ml) chicken broth
1 teaspoon (5 ml) dried herb blend
¼ cup (55 g/half of a stick) butter
  or stick margarine

6 cups (215 g) dry cubed bread
  (see sidebar)
½ cup (120 ml/50 g) coarsely
  chopped pecans
1 small apple (peeled or not, as you
  prefer), diced

Spray inside of slow cooker generously with nonstick spray; set aside. In large skillet, cook sausage over medium heat, stirring frequently to break up, until some of the fat is rendered. Add celery and onion and continue to cook, stirring frequently, until meat is no longer pink and vegetables are tender-crisp, about 5 minutes. Remove from heat; drain and discard excess grease. Add broth and herb blend to skillet, stirring to mix.

In Dutch oven, melt butter over medium heat. Add bread cubes and cook until golden brown, stirring frequently. Remove from heat. Add pecans, apple, and sausage mixture from skillet; stir well to combine. Transfer mixture to prepared slow cooker. Cover and cook on low for 4 hours, or on high for 2 hours; the dressing can cook up to 5 hours on low.

 MAKING BREAD CUBES FOR DRESSING

When you're preparing recipes that call for cubed dry bread, you could use prepackaged unseasoned stuffing cubes, but it's best to make your own bread cubes. Cut a denser bread, like French or Italian bread, into 3/4- to 1-inch (2 to 2.5 cm) cubes. Spread them out on a baking sheet and let them dry overnight, stirring several times if possible. If you're in a hurry, spread the cubes out in a single layer on a baking sheet, and bake in a 300°F (150°C) oven until dry and crisp, about 20 minutes.

LATE-SUMMER SUCCOTASH

6 servings
Prep: 15 minutes
Cooking: 5 hours on low, or 3 hours on high (can cook up to 7 hours on low)
Slow cooker: Small or Standard

Succotash comes to us from the early Native Americans; its name derives from the Narragansett word *msickquatash,* which translates to "boiled whole-kernel corn." There are many versions of succotash today; this one uses fresh corn for an extra-sweet flavor.

4 whole ears fresh corn-on-the-cob
Half of a can (10¾ ounces/305 g can size) condensed cream of celery soup
**   (reduced-fat works fine)**
½ cup (120 ml) chicken broth
1 package (9 ounces/255 g) frozen lima beans, thawed
1 red bell pepper, cut into ½-inch (1.25 cm) cubes
Half of a small onion, diced
2 cloves garlic, minced
1 bay leaf
½ teaspoon (2.5 ml) dried marjoram leaves
¼ teaspoon (1.25 ml) salt
A few grindings of black pepper
Chopped fresh parsley

Cut kernels off corncobs; add kernels and any corn milk from the cutting board to slow cooker. Hold each cut cob over the slow cooker, and use a table knife to scrape the milky juices into the slow cooker; discard cobs as each is scraped. Add remaining ingredients except parsley to slow cooker; stir to mix well. Cover and cook on low for 5 hours, or on high for 3 hours; succotash can cook up to 7 hours on low. Before serving, discard bay leaf; sprinkle with fresh parsley.

VARIATION: SUCCOTASH WITH GAME
Follow recipe above, adding ½ pound (225 g) finely diced bear meat to slow cooker with other ingredients. Or, you could add the same amount of smoked venison sausage, cut into ½-inch (1.25 cm) cubes. Proceed as directed.

INDEX

Creative Publishing international
is your complete source for fish and wild game cookbooks.

Available cooking titles:

- America's Favorite Fish Recipes
- America's Favorite Wild Game Recipes
- Babe & Kris Winkelman's
  Great Fish & Game Recipes
- Backyard Grilling
- Cooking Wild in Kate's Camp
- Cooking Wild in Kate's Kitchen
- Dressing & Cooking Wild Game
- Game Bird Cookery
- The New Cleaning & Cooking Fish
- Preparing Fish & Wild Game
- Recipes from Nature
- The Saltwater Cookbook
- Venison Cookery

To purchase these or other titles,
contact your local bookseller, or visit our
website at **www.creativepub.com.**

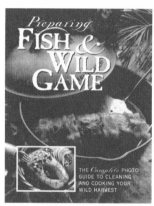
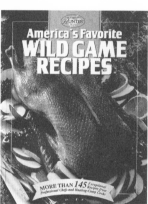